The Diaconate and Marriage

The Diaconate and Marriage

Deacon James Keating, PhD

Our Sunday Visitor
Huntington, Indiana

Nihil Obstat
Msgr. Michael Heintz, Ph.D.
Censor Librorum

Imprimatur
✠ Kevin C. Rhoades
Bishop of Fort Wayne-South Bend
July 21, 2025

The *Nihil Obstat* and *Imprimatur* are official declarations that a book is free from doctrinal or moral error. It is not implied that those who have granted the *Nihil Obstat* and *Imprimatur* agree with the contents, opinions, or statements expressed.

31 30 29 28 27 26   1 2 3 4 5 6 7 8 9

Our Sunday Visitor Publishing Division
Our Sunday Visitor, Inc.
200 Noll Plaza
Huntington, IN 46750
www.osv.com
1-800-348-2440

ISBN: 978-1-63966-385-9 (Inventory No. T3009)

1. RELIGION—Christianity—Catholic—General.
2. RELIGION—Clergy.
3. RELIGION—Christian Living—Love & Marriage.

eISBN: 978-1-63966-386-6
LCCN: 2025942811

Cover and interior design: Amanda Falk
Cover art: Adobe Stock

PRINTED IN THE UNITED STATES OF AMERICA

Contents

Foreword

The vocation of the permanent diaconate is a gift to the Church that stands as both a profound expression of Christ's servanthood and a tangible witness to His sacrificial love. Nowhere is this vocation more evident than in the lives of married deacons, whose ministry and marriage converge to become a living icon of Christ's love for His Church. In this book, Deacon James Keating delves deeply into this sacred convergence, presenting a compelling theological and pastoral exploration of how these two sacraments mutually enrich and strengthen one another.

As a brother in the diaconate, I have had the privilege of collaborating with Deacon Keating through shared writing projects, mutual reviews, and numerous speaking engagements. What has always impressed me about his approach is the way he weaves together theological insight, pastoral sensitivity, and practical application to address the most pressing needs of the diaconal community. In this book, he offers not only a framework for understanding the profound connection between marriage and ordination but also a spiritual vision that invites married deacons and their spouses into a deeper communion with Christ and with one another.

At the heart of *The Diaconate and Marriage* lies a theme that resonates deeply with the spirituality of the diaconate: the primacy of sacramental grace in sustaining both ministry and marriage. Keating beautifully articulates how the married deacon becomes a sign of Christ's spousal and diaconal love, a love that is simultaneously self-giving and service oriented. Drawing from the Trinitarian life of love and communion, he challenges readers to view their vocations as rooted in the sacramental life, where grace transforms the ordinary into the extraordinary.

What makes this book especially timely is the increasing need for an integrated understanding of diaconal ministry within the broader context of family life. Too often, formation programs treat marriage and ordination as parallel but disconnected realities, failing to account for the ways in which these sacraments shape and sustain one another. Keating addresses this gap with theological depth and pastoral clarity, offering a vision that calls both deacons and their spouses to embrace their shared vocation as co-ministers of Christ's love. His exploration of how the Eucharist serves as the source and summit of both marriage and ministry is particularly illuminating, grounding his insights in the very heart of the Church's sacramental life.

One of the book's most compelling aspects is its practical approach to the lived reality of married deacons. Keating does not shy away from addressing the challenges that arise when ministry strains family life or when the demands of marriage seem to conflict with those of diaconal service. Instead, he provides practical guidance for navigating these tensions with prayer, intentionality, and grace. His call for a life of mutual discernment, shared prayer, and ongoing communication between husband and wife is both inspiring and actionable, making this work an invaluable resource for couples seeking to grow in their vocation together.

Moreover, Keating's emphasis on formation stands out as a prophetic invitation to rethink how the Church prepares men and their wives for this unique vocation. By highlighting the importance of spiritual maturity, affective depth, and the centrality of the interior life, he sets a high bar for what diaconal formation can and should be. His reflections on the role of the wife in discerning and sustaining a husband's vocation are particularly timely, offering a much-needed corrective to approaches that often overlook her vital participation in the diaconal call.

For married deacons and their spouses, this book has the potential to be transformative. It invites them into a deeper awareness of how their sacramental lives are intertwined, calling them to reflect more fully the mystery of Christ's love for His Bride. For those in diaconal formation, it serves as a road map for navigating the complexities of integrating ministry and marriage. For the wider Church, it provides a vision of the diaconate that is both inspiring and grounded, reminding us all of the profound ways in which God works through the sacramental lives of ordinary men and women.

In these pages, Deacon Keating offers more than just a theological treatise or a pastoral guide; he offers a vision of what it means to live as a sacramental sign of Christ's love in a world that desperately needs it. May his insights inspire and transform all who read this book, drawing them closer to Christ and to one another in the service of His Church.

Deacon Dominic Cerrato, Ph.D.
November 2024

Introduction

Marriage in Christ and the ordination of a man into the servant mysteries of Christ as a deacon form an integral sign. This sign points to what the Bridegroom-Servant Christ enacted in the Incarnation. The Sacrament of Matrimony images Christ's loving His Bride, the Church; and the Sacrament of Holy Orders allows Christ to continue His ministerial presence, serving the spiritual and corporal needs of humanity. Together, these two sacraments come together in the body of the one man, the spouse-deacon. When the sacraments come together in this way, a married deacon becomes a sign of Christ's *own spousal commitment* even unto death and a sign that such love for wife and Church (marriage, Eph 5:31–33) manifests itself in concrete service to his wife's real needs and the real needs of parishioners (diaconal ministry). Behind these two sacraments lies that which was hidden but is now revealed: Love and service have their origin in the inner life of the Holy Trinity. This life, shrouded and impossible to penetrate with reason alone, was revealed in the flesh of Christ during His time on earth. What was revealed is simple: God is an eternal circulation of love within a relational bond of persons: Father, Son, and Holy Spirit.

Thus, the life and ministry of Christ became a window into this circulation of love. And our entry into the sacramental life keeps this window open. Each deacon draws his capacity to love from the power of sacramental grace, just as each husband and wife do. This grace is a participation in the love and life of God. Participating in this vocational grace, deacons and spouses become holy. Such sanctity is a witness, eliciting wonder in others as they see fruit in the character and action of those being configured to Christ. Every act Christ performed drew its beginning and purpose from His relatedness to the Divine Persons of the Holy Trinity. In other words, Christ's service to humanity flows from a supernatural and eternal reservoir of love that is the relationships within the Most Holy Trinity.

Such an endless source of love fuels miraculous resuscitations of bodies, healings of wounds and limbs, restoring of sight to eyes, as well as Christ's myriad spiritual and corporal works of mercy. The coming of Christ into the world was the unveiling of the source of all goodness and holiness: "Our Father, who art in heaven." From this source, Christ drew life and power. It is this source that eventually raised Him from the dead. He was so embedded in communion with this source of eternal life and love that He could never be defined by death. Death had to release Him — and now releases those who participate in Christ's life through the sacraments.

As a man configured to the servant mysteries of Christ through ordination, a deacon is called to draw his life and ministry from this same divine source. Objectively, the deacon's ministry is a participation in those same spiritual and corporal works of mercy that formed Christ's own ministry. Subjectively, the deacon remains with Christ in ministry through the promptings of the Spirit in his conscience. A well-formed deacon is a man who lives in communion with Christ so that Christ can communicate His own actions to him. This deacon lives Christ's own charity, Christ's own prayer and worship, Christ's own nuptial generosity toward the Church, Christ's own obedience to the Father, Christ's own freedom from "this age" (Rom 12:2). The deacon, through his formation in holy orders, his renunciation of mortal sin, and his vulnerability to the objective grace of ordination, offers his body as a locus for Christ's own actions. In other words, the deacon practices a sacramental ministry. The deacon is tapping into Christ as his source of identity and ministry. As Christ shares His own life and love with the deacon, a ministry of consequences flows. Such consequences occur if the deacon subjectively abides with Christ through contemplative prayer, Eucharistic devotion, and the crucifying choice to allow Christ's healing prayer to effect conversion upon conversion.

What further contextualizes the participation of the deacon in the life and love of Christ's own communion with the Father and the Spirit is the deacon's sacramental marriage. Of course, there are celibate and widowed deacons, but for the purposes of this book, I am focusing on married deacons. Receiving diaconal grace into an already established sacramental marriage profoundly orients the witness of the deacon and his spouse to the depths of God's own identity as an eternal circulation of love. Deacon and spouse are called into a fascination with this circulation of love. It was this circulating divine love that overflowed into time by way of the Incarnation and the sending of the Holy Spirit at Pentecost, and it continues to do so, always in and through the sacramental life of the Church. In Christ, both the man in holy orders and the marriage he shares with his spouse become a revelation of hidden truths. The source of this man's ministry, Christ's own envoy-servant identity (Jn 13:15) pulses through him. And in this man's marriage, the power of Christ's own love for the Church is revealed.

Over time, as the deacon-husband draws the strength of his spousal and ministerial actions from the supernatural, he matures into a clearer sign of the Bridegroom-Servant Christ. Locating the meaning of his vocation deep within the Eucharist as its origin and sustenance, the deacon-husband comes to know Christ giving himself away in love in the hope of an ongoing holy exchange of loves. From Calvary, and now re-presented sacramentally in the Mass and in Christian marriage, Christ entrusts His body to the one He loves, His Bride, the Church. The deacon, through all the sacraments he has received, and now in holy orders, participates in Christ's own self-donative love, expressing such a love in both marriage and ministerial service.

To remain so open to Christ's actions now enfleshed in his own, the deacon-husband needs to consent to a life of prayer. Only such a subjective commitment will keep him in communion with the objective reality he entered on his wedding and ordination days. Neither sacrament "magically" endures; both are relationally sustained. To prolong one's life of communion with God and spouse, a deacon must become and remain a man of communication. Such communication guards and deepens the intimacy between himself and recipients of his love: God and wife. The deacon learns this way of communion from the revelation of Christ himself, who did not simply enter prayer with His Father but, in fact, became prayer. Christ's whole life was one of ceaseless intimacy with God (1 Thes 5:17). It can be said that Christ himself *is communication.*[*]

In other words, Christ is the revelation that the Trinity is an exchange of Persons in love, relations that remain open to be affected by the Others and given to the Others as their very being. The more a deacon subjectively commits to prayer, the more he allows vulnerable communication to become his way of being.

* Joseph Ratzinger, *Behold the Pierced One: An Approach to a Spiritual Christology* (Ignatius Press, 1986), 25–26.

In prayer and regular participation in the Eucharist, the deacon expresses his desire to be affected by the very way God is God: a reciprocal love that is a bond generating spiritual fruit.[†] The deacon-husband wants to join his yes to marriage and ministerial service to the yes Christ gives to His Father and the Spirit. This yes is Christ's consent to serve the needs of suffering persons. So deep were these affirmations to the Father and the Spirit in service to suffering humanity that when He consented to the Cross, in obedience to love, He wed divinity to suffering humanity. Such union with suffering humanity truly birthed hope in us, whom He loves as His spouse. The deacon's yes to all that ministry and marriage calls him to can be sustained for a lifetime only when espoused to Christ's own yes, Christ's own obedience.

Celibacy

In effect, the deacon has become a revelation of the Bridegroom Christ — first, through his own marriage and, second, by way of his service to the needs of Christ's Bride, the Church. As such, he begins to understand why priests remain celibate and take Christ's interest, the welfare of the Church, as their sole interest. Such celibate living can flow only from the deepest Eucharistically charged contemplative prayer. As the deacon becomes more Christlike, more holy, through this life of prayer and service, it becomes clearer to him why the Church requires celibacy even of him, if his wife were to predecease him. This diaconal celibacy can become prophetic for the rest of the Church.

As an invigorating expression of such a sign, widowed deacons might consider banding together in community. They would become a group of men prophetically embodying the future of the whole Church in heaven. This embodiment is celibate, as those in heaven "neither marry nor are given in marriage" (Mt 22:30). In heaven, one is spousally fascinated with the eternal,

† See Cardinal Angelo Scola, *The Nuptial Mystery* (Eerdmans, 2005), 103.

the Holy Trinity, as his first interest. Such a celibate life of sharing in communal prayer and fellowship until death would capstone a life of sharing in Christ's own mystery of self-donative service. Today, many widowed deacons live lives that are too isolated, even removed from ministry and diocesan life, sidelined by the tragic deaths of their wives. To gather in such a community would console these deacons and signal the Church's true destiny as espoused to God alone.

Formation

Such a rich vocation as described above, either in marriage or as a celibate, needs substantive and intentional formation. Hopefully, as we grow in deeper awareness of the Christological heart of the diaconate, the Church's mandated formation content will be reassessed. I do not believe diaconal formation needs to be any longer than three years, with a propaedeutic year to transition men out of being formed by the popular and political American culture into men being formed in Catholic sensibility and interiority.* The deacon does not need to be formed in a mini seminary academic program. The deacon's mission is simpler and has no need of all the coursework in which a seminarian engages. Diaconal formation should concentrate on gaining competency in Scripture studies primarily, along with studies in spirituality, liturgy, pastoral theology, moral theology, sacramental theology (especially regarding marriage), and all the practicums necessary for preaching, liturgical assistance and presiding, visiting the sick and the imprisoned, and aiding engaged and married couples. In place of a more extensive academic schedule, the three years should be filled with formation in human development and maturity, spiritual practices, and pastoral experience

* This recommendation is in accord with the *National Directory for the Formation, Ministry, and Life of Permanent Deacons in the USA*, 2nd Edition (USCCB, 2021), n. 214. The Directory mandates two years of aspirancy, but based upon my experience I do believe that only one propaedeutic year is necessary.

and supervision. Any topic not covered in the three years can be offered in ongoing formation after ordination.

Further, I believe that all formation must become residential. We can no longer afford to denigrate formation as an exclusively "post-work" program of evening courses. What we need are full weekend formation programs once, or even twice, a month, augmented by summer weeklong formation for marriage enrichment, liturgical intensives, prayer formation, and priest-deacon collaboration training. Within this kind of timeframe and concentration, husband and wife may begin to fully discern what Christ is inviting them to participate in for the rest of their lives. The particulars of such a formation revolution must be left to individual dioceses, but I believe we cannot go forward and sustain the diaconate with formation being "business as usual."

Prescinding from a more concentrated reflection upon both the formation of deacons and the lifestyle of widowed deacons, let me turn toward and focus upon the vocation of diaconal life in marriage. This vocation is a share in Christ's own ministry and nuptial love.

CHAPTER 1
The Call

In love, the spouse comes seeking the beloved. One sees or receives the gaze of the other and, in so seeing or receiving, is awakened. Love brings us to life. Romantic love is an ecstasy with a cross buried in it. This ecstasy is thrilling. "God has said it is not good for me to be alone — and now I am not!" Being seen by the opposite sex leads to a self that yields its own self-involvement to a life of serving the real needs of another. In other words, that aspect of the self that is egocentric is crucified by presence and commitment. Ecstasy is short-lived in marriage. Bachelors tend to choose actions that bathe the ego in natural consolation. These activities usually carry the motivation of self-involvement; they are instigated by what "I want." The woman calls out to the bachelor to understand himself, instead, as a bestowed gift. Love invites a new understanding of the self as one who is given and giving. It is *this* man whom the woman calls and invites to remain with her. Love, through presence and commitment, bids the man to be awakened and conscious of himself as one who can possess himself only by giving himself away in love.

Love pleads with the husband to guard this emerging self as a gift and not let the self-involved ego rule again. Love, in other words, tries to reach and encourage the self that is Christ ("Yet I live, no longer I, but Christ lives in me" [Gal 2:20]) to emerge and remain in an unfolding and lasting love.

Becoming Christ is the vocation of a husband (Eph 5:25). Receiving such selfless love from her husband is the vocation of the bride, to which she responds by giving herself completely. "And there will be one Christ, loving himself," as Saint Augustine writes.* As we love our spouses in Christ, He increasingly is identified with us, and as us. "Whatever you did for one of these least brothers of mine, you did for me" (Mt 25:40). We can also see this identification becoming real each time we receive holy Communion. With our "amen," we consent to have His Body become more and more ours and our body become more and more His. "Christ is all and in all" (Col 3:11). Such is the spousal nature of Christianity.

"The relationship between the man-woman and Christ-church pairs is now so closely linked that each of the two mysteries can be understood only in the light of the other."† Sacramental marriage can be understood only by considering Christ and His own spousal self-emptying on the Cross. It is such self-emptying that is celebrated, re-presented, and participated in when any man and woman enter sacramental marriage. This marriage receives its meaning from the Eucharistic Liturgy; Calvary becomes resurrection celebrated in signs and symbols. The Mass is a wedding, and all other weddings that want to flourish receive their orienting truth and sufficient power by yielding to

* "There shall be one Christ, loving himself. For when the members love one another, the body loves itself. … Now you are the body of Christ, and members. When therefore you love members of Christ, you love Christ; when you love Christ, you love the Son of God; when you love the Son of God, you love also the Father. The love therefore cannot be separated into parts." Homily 10, on the First Epistle of John, par. 3 (1 Jn 5:1).

† Scola, *The Nuptial Mystery*, 77.

the Mass and surrendering in participation to the Mass's same action: "The Son of Man did not come to be served but to serve" (Mt 20:28). Within marriage hides not only a cross but a diaconal-shaped cross. Within the Mass is Christ sharing with His Bride, the Church, His own *diakonia*, His ministry of self-forgetfulness.

All the baptized are called to mount this diaconal cross of service, of self-forgetfulness in the face of human need, and so be affected by and respond to human suffering. But only the deacon is called to be configured to this aspect of Christ's own spousal self-donation and enflesh it *liturgically*. In the Liturgy, at the ambo, and as he assists the priest at the altar, the deacon reveals through prayer and proclamation the servant mysteries of Christ. These mysteries then extend themselves to those in need by way of the deacon's body ministering beyond the altar. The deacon is the only other person besides the priest who can speak the very words of Jesus during liturgical prayer. This is why he is ordained. He can be Christ's voice in the Liturgy as salvation is being proclaimed and offered.[‡] Christ inhabits the voice of the deacon, and through him, Christ continues to reveal His mission of self-donation in every age. The deacon is to possess an eager availability not simply to speak the words of Christ but to enflesh them in action when the Liturgy has concluded.

Attraction to Ministry

To enter this mystery of being one who proclaims the servant mysteries of Christ, one must first possess a desire to know who Christ is, an attraction to His identity and mission. In light of this desire, the Church will then confirm whether that man possesses sufficient character to become a bridge to Christ for oth-

‡ "When the Sacred Scriptures are read in the Church, God himself speaks to his people, and Christ, present in his word, proclaims the Gospel." United States Conference of Catholic Bishops (USCCB), *General Instruction of the Roman Missal*, par. 29.

ers. Many times, it is not the Church — meaning parish clergy or parishioners — that first recognizes the presence of this character but the man's spouse. She may approach her husband and ask if he ever noticed an attraction to ordination. After this, many conversations on discernment commence. After a husband expresses interest in ordination, a wife may be both frightened and attracted to such a reality.

What sometimes attracts the wife to having a husband in holy orders is her own love of God and the potential for a deepening of the Faith within them as a couple and with their children. What often instills fear in her is the time commitment demanded of a man in holy orders. Will his seeking of holy orders be a threat to the couple's intimacy, communication, and shared presence?

Is her fear warranted? It could be so if the diocese does not screen out affectively immature men, or men who confuse "doing more" with a commitment to God. Affective immaturity manifests itself as activism in many men. This type of man needs to see progress in his résumé, an accumulation of achievements giving him an identity that others can admire. He has set his eye on the diaconate as his next acquisition. Such a man would, indeed, threaten the stability of his marriage if he added yet another round of activities to his already busy life. The greater issue, however, is that the marriage is already threatened by the commitments engaging him, those fueling his cultural, but not his theological, identity.

The wife's fear could also be warranted if she knows there is a weak link in her husband's faith life that has remained unspoken between her and her husband. Perhaps she knows that her husband has little or no prayer life. He does not read Scripture or engage in spiritual reading. He has little interest in the Mass beyond attending on Sunday, and there are other such indications that he lacks a lively interior life. With such a void, could he really be called to holy orders? The wife may also know of defects in his life of virtue that ought to be strengthened before any inquiry or application to enter holy orders is initiated. Finally, her fears may be well founded because his paternal commitment is weak, and he possesses a strained relationship with his children. All these things and more would be enough for her fears to be reasonable.

Therefore, one of the first steps any diocese should take in considering a man's inquiry at the vocation office is substantive feedback from the wife. I think questions such as the following would aid any director of deacons and his bishop to discern whether an application should be granted:

- Please describe your husband's prayer life.
- How often do you and your husband speak together at a level that intimately bonds you?
- Have you ever felt lonely in your marriage? Why or why not?
- Describe your husband's understanding of fatherhood. Describe how his fatherhood is concretely expressed.
- What is your husband's weakness regarding his ability to make you know you are loved and secure?
- What aspect of your husband's personality is off-putting to you or others?
- When did your husband last go to confession?
- Do you and your husband ever pray together outside of attending Mass? How is this prayer structured? How often do the two of you pray? For how long do you pray?
- What was the last spiritual book your husband read?
- What emotions (anger, envy, egocentric ambition, lust, sadness, etc.) displayed by your husband to-

ward you or others most concern you, and why?

- Would you say your husband is a hard worker? What does this mean to you? How is this behavior expressed? If he is not a hard worker, what has he accomplished that has helped to enhance your love for him?
- Would you describe your husband as a loner? Does he have any close male friends?
- Does your husband have to be the center of attention at parties?
- When was the last time someone sought your husband out for advice regarding a personal or important matter? How did you feel about this?
- Does your husband demonstrate that your marriage is a top priority in his life? Give a recent example.
- How often is your husband out of the home each week because of job responsibilities? How often is he out of the house due to parish commitments or volunteering opportunities?
- How many hours a week does your husband work?
- Do you have any concerns regarding your husband's ability to integrate family life with diaconal responsibilities?
- Have you ever witnessed your husband drunk in public or under the influence of illegal drugs? If yes, describe the circumstances as you know them.
- Do you have knowledge that your husband has viewed pornography within the last two years? If yes, describe the circumstances as you know them.
- Does your husband exhibit the virtue of chastity in his words and behavior?
- Have you ever been embarrassed or humiliated by your husband's behavior in public? If yes, please de-

scribe the circumstances.

- How receptive is your husband to criticism from you? From authority?
- Has your husband ever emotionally or physically abused you? If so, what are the circumstances of the abuse?
- Is there a pattern of demeaning behavior toward you from your husband (e.g., he minimizes your opinions, teases you excessively, makes you the butt of jokes, is sarcastic toward you, interrupts your speaking as a pattern, etc.)?
- Do you see priests respecting your husband?
- How will your friends and family react when they learn your husband is in diaconal formation?
- Why do you remain a Catholic?

Recognizing that the husband possesses a growing desire to seek ordination, the diocese also must consult his wife. Does the wife have any attraction to living in a diaconal marriage? She may, in fact, experience a real draw to welcoming the vocation of holy orders into her marriage. Recognizing the legitimate fear noted earlier in this chapter, I will now consider that welcoming holy orders into a marriage can be very attractive. Building upon her emotionally mature and spiritually intimate relationship with her husband, a wife may detect that this call will bring both her and her husband even closer to God and to one another. The process of formation, she anticipates, could be the occasion for deepening all the good that is already present within their solid commitment to each other. In discussion with other wives or deacons, she is encouraged to follow her attraction and to share with her husband the content of her vision of what life in a diaconal marriage would look like. God shares His will with us by deepening our desire for the good He is inviting. Detecting an attraction to such a gift as holy orders comingling with her marriage has an appeal worth praying and seeking spiritual direction about.

Conversely, the Church and the husband must be cautious about any wife who may initiate the process for a man to seek ordination — cautious in the sense that she may want it more than he does. As a man might want to add holy orders to his résumé, a woman might want her husband to become a deacon for immature or self-involved reasons. In this scenario, having a husband who is a deacon would raise her worth in the eyes of the local church; she would see it as her chance to stand out, to possess an identity that is admired by others in the community. This immature initiation of a vocation is different from that of a wife who supports her husband's attraction. It may even be that sometimes a wife sees a deacon in her husband before he does. To mention this "seeing" to the husband is different from her encouraging him to explore it for her self-involved reasons.

In all this, we know that the pursuit of a vocation may carry mixed motives. Having a pure motive igniting our choices in any one of our hearts is rare. Yes, one ought to want to be a deacon to become a herald of the Gospel, but he also may derive some pleasure from entering the clerical state and increasing in stature within the parish community. "Yes, mostly I want my husband to be a deacon who is generous in self-giving, but I enjoy being proud of his leadership and his gifts as a reflection on me as well." These more subtle motives lacking purity can be healed during the formation process. In fact, that is one of the reasons formation exists: to heal the movement of our relentless egos, which try their best to take center stage even in a commitment that, by its very nature, is about serving others through the grace of God.

Detecting a Call

Each man called to the diaconate receives the vocation in a personal way. Nevertheless, there are some common elements displayed in all vocations. First, it is common in discerning a clerical vocation that a man notices an ever-greater attraction to spiritual things, such as prayer and Scripture reading, and a new eagerness to renounce sin and embrace virtue.

Second, it is usual to notice a growing interest in what the Church is interested in. A man becomes more fascinated with leading people to God and grows in his desire to pray with people and for them. He notices a new or expanding attraction to evangelize, to be a public Catholic.

Third, there begins or deepens a draw toward more frequent participation in the Liturgy. It is common for a man called to the diaconate to find himself more and more present at daily Mass, even at a cost. For example, he may find himself motivated to worship at the 6:00 a.m. daily Mass so he can make it to work on time.

Fourth, a man will find himself desiring to read about the meaning of ordination, what it is to live a clerical life. Here, he is sensing that something is missing in the way he is living Catholicism. He wonders if there is more. What this more is has something to do with serving the mission of the Church more closely. This fourth point is closely related to the third and first attractions. In short, a man who is called to the diaconate wants to be with God *more*!

These four initial attractions common to a clerical vocation are simply the concretization of that universal human desire to spend one's life in the presence of God. In Mark 3:14, we read, "He appointed twelve [whom he also named apostles] that they might be with him, and he might send them forth to preach." The essence of clerical formation is embedded in this most succinct summary of what such formation entails. A man called to holy orders wants to be configured to Christ *by living with Him*. One purpose of living with Christ, of "being with Him," is to ultimately be sent by Him so that His own mission can be extended in the current age. Only out of such communion with Christ is a man then sent into ministry. If there is no communion, no being with Christ, there can be no authentic sending. Holy Orders is the fruit of knowing Christ and being sent by Him because of this knowing. Further and most vital, such knowledge is mediated by the Church. So no man can rightly have a vocation if he is not desirous of prayer (communion with Christ) and if this prayer life does not have its source in the Church. To be ordained is to have the Church as one's first communal allegiance and true home.

Discerning a call to holy orders means gaining an awareness that "my" way of loving Christ is best embraced within a public configuration to His ministry. Being a cleric will facilitate my dependence on His grace and keep me in communion with God through prayer. A call, a vocation, is ultimately *one's way* of being saved from sin. Coming to understand a vocation as "my" way of more easily becoming a saint is not an isolating "my" but a personalizing of one's foundational ecclesial membership. God does not call the masses; God does not call one as a generic human being; God calls *thou*. This is why discernment even exists; each person must hear his own name called. The Church does not want volunteers to enter holy orders. The Church wants men who know God and know they are known by Him.

Recruitment?

One final comment on discernment: Note how personal the call is. On occasion, however, one may have his vocation "kick-started" by members of the Church mentioning that they see a deacon in a man. This is good, and it may be the beginning of an authentic vocation. Nevertheless, all that such prophetic voicing indicates is that now discernment must begin *for that man.* A vocation is *not* born of recruitment. There are some deacons who think part of their vocation is to go around trying to get as many men as possible into diaconal formation. Holy orders is not the military, the Boy Scouts, a golf league, or a private men's club, all of which want bodies to fill empty slots or spaces. The Church does not need deacons in this way. The Church needs deacons not to fill in the ranks but to answer a perceived call from God. A man in relation to the Most Holy Trinity finds his way into his vocation; he is not recruited as a strategy. To reduce a vocation to recruitment is to risk having deacons who are motivated to please others or who feel "special" or "singled out." No, the men the Church needs are those who feel wonder, surprise, humility, and awe that *their prayer life has led them to desire attachment to the word of God and the altar, bearing fruit in public ministry.*

Priests may seem like recruiters at times, as they do actively contact chanceries or deacon directors to find more men to become deacons because they need "help." Asking for relief from pastoral duties is understandable, but the baptized can also bring Communion to the sick or make hospital or nursing home visits to pray with and console residents there. Why do they need a man in holy orders to help in this way? I am hoping that someday priests will request a deacon not simply because they need relief from pastoral work but because they desire to have a brother cleric to pray with, envision the parish's future, cultivate evangelization as a parish mission, and form parishioners in a school of prayer. Someday, perhaps, more seminaries will collaborate with deacon-formation processes to form priests who want such deacons and to form deacons who become such brothers to priests. We must reject reducing deacons to pastoral functionaries.

To speed this day in arriving, two things must happen: First, seminaries need to form seminarians into deacons and no longer see the diaconate as simply a year in which a future priest gets practice in preaching and pastoral presence, as well as when he commits to celibacy. Second, deacon formation must become more selective in accepting candidates into formation. If deacons want to be collaborators, they must present themselves to priests as formed in a deeper level of conversion and competency. A deacon needs to be a churchman who can imagine a new vision of ministry along with the pastor. Deacons must bring more Catholicity to the table if they are to be seen as brothers in holy orders. By this, I mean the men who come out of diaconal formation must possess an ecclesial mind, a theological heart, and a pastoral prudence that can truly be an asset to a bishop and his mission, in communion with the priests with whom he ministers.

Marriage and Discernment

So, if the call to becoming a deacon is personal, a man should first communicate his desire to respond to that call with his most personal friend: his wife. There have been cases in which the wife is the last to know about these desires. In these backward cases, men have spoken to their parish priest, deacons, counselors, work colleagues, and even parents to test responses to his seeking ordination. The first two questions any priest (or other adviser) should ask a man who approaches seeking assistance in vocational discernment are these: What did God say in prayer? What did your wife say? If the man does not know the answer to these two questions, teach him how to pray, and ask him about the emotional and moral condition of his marriage.

When bringing the desire for ordination out into the open for discussion with one's wife, there are a few elements to keep in mind:

- Go gently in revealing your attraction to holy orders. You may have been thinking and praying about your attraction for a long time. You may be excited about telling your wife, imagining her to be as excited as you are. This is *not* her vocation, so she may not be excited at all. She may be cautious or, depending on your life together, even incredulous ("Another thing to add to our lives?"). Let her receive this desire of yours in the way she can now. If she receives your news with some negativity or hesitancy, simply ask her to think about it and confirm with her that you can discuss it again in a few days. From the husband's point of view, entering formation may seem positive and a good thing for himself, but the wife may be calculating its effects upon the relationship. In one case, a man approached his wife to discuss his applying for the diaconate, and her response was curt but accurate: "Diaconate? You are not even a good husband." It is vital that no man attempt to incorporate the diaconate into a sacramental marriage if his spousal commitment is anything but vigorous and mature.

- If your wife is positive about your inquiry into a vocation to holy orders from the outset, then it would be a good time to lay out what you have discovered about the time demands placed upon a candidate in formation. It would also be good to discuss any of her questions or concerns about the vocation. It might be good to see if your diocese is holding any public meetings for husbands and wives interested in the diaconate to attend together. Many questions are answered in such gatherings. If children are present in the marriage, you and your wife should consider the best time to include them in the conversation. The children need to get a sense of how their lives will change as well. Having a father become a public religious person can be very stressful for some children. Some children of deacons have been teased by friends about their "priest dad." Of course, other children's experiences are more positive, and they feel proud to have a father who ministers at the altar on Sundays. (I will say more about the children's situation in chapters 3 and 4.)

- Whatever the wife's initial reaction to her husband's exploration into a diaconal vocation, both spouses should move toward an intentional commitment to enter discerning prayer. This should entail a commitment to prayer both together and on one's own. Over days of prayer, the Holy Spirit will begin to open courage where it is needed. This courage may embolden a wife to tell her husband that the marriage is not strong enough to receive holy orders into it. Or the Spirit may flood her heart with peace as a sign that the marriage is strong and generous enough to enfold the diaconal mission within it. During these days of intentional prayer, it may be helpful for both spouses to seek advice from their pastor or a mature deacon with a prayer life to test what they are hearing in prayer. Neither spouse should consult a "cheerleader" for the diaconate but, rather, men and women whom they judge to be persons with a lively interior life, not possessing an agenda in favor of the diaconate but simply desiring the marriage to reach its potential in holiness.

Marriage is a form of hospitality. It is a choice to "make room" for another and for that other to become one's first interest. Having one man or woman as a first interest is spousal commitment. As a result of this hospitality, spouses are then asked to become even more generous and welcome children as the fruit of their nuptial love. All this openness to life and otherness is contextualized in the more fundamental hosting we do toward God. God is the Eternal Spouse of us all; we are destined to be welcomed into His own life through the life of the Bridegroom Christ for all eternity. This is the destiny of our present marriages as their meaning fully opens to the eternal union with God that they prefigure in time.

Some couples not only open their hearts to receive God and their spouse and children, but they are also invited to receive the Sacrament of Holy Orders into their spousal commitment. What they are welcoming is a sign of Christ's own envoy-servant identity. This sign is entrusted to the man who is called to the diaconate, but it is also one that his spouse and children participate in by way of their own faith and generosity. Christ is asking a husband and father, "May I inhabit your body in such a way as to proclaim amid the Church that my attraction to human pain and suffering, my attraction to evangelizing and praying, has not left the earth? May I live my mystery of service and proclamation and prayer over again in your body?" Being part of the life of a man who hears this invitation from Christ can be frightening, but over time, hopefully, it will become consoling. Embedded within the family now is a man who finds himself called again not only to spousal and paternal love but also to keeping the grace of Christological service alive in his time. If such a call is authentic, it can only be a grace to any marriage.

CHAPTER 2

The Ending of Idol Worship: Formation

After a diaconal vocation is well discerned, both the husband and the wife must commit to a surprising element of their marriage. They must be further formed into spouses, but beyond the content of engagement retreats and seminars or couple mentoring. Now, building upon those formative processes and whatever years of marriage have passed since their engagement, they are to be formed anew in a mission that keeps their spousal love central but orients it into an ecclesial life of public ministry. When this is done well, its result is usually more beautiful than any couple could imagine. In what at first might have been construed as a threat to marriage, adding the element of holy orders is now seen as a special sign of love given to the couple by God to strengthen their marriage. They are strengthened by a deeper commitment to Christ to resist former habits of idolatry.

By *idolatry*, I mean those realities one turns to instead of God in times of suffering or in seeking rest or pleasure. As a result of quality ministerial formation, the couple has turned from any idols still lingering in their lives. They now commit themselves to fully face only the real God in worship. He is the one and only reality from which they now draw ultimate meaning, consolation, healing, and virtue. All other previous sources of idolatry found in entertainment, finances, career, pleasure, and power simply remain as instrumental and functional. Having once bent these realities into idols, those idols now stand revealed as superficial and passing. At the end of diaconal formation that is done correctly, the couple fall more in love with one another and with God as revealed in Christ and celebrated in the Eucharist.

This destruction of idolatry is the real grace of having been fully present to the content and processes of formation for holy orders. As theologian David Fagerberg writes:

> The Second Vatican Council recovered the permanent diaconate order, dedicated to liturgy, word and charity. The deacon is not primarily a server of food, but is, rather, a minister of the mysteries of Jesus Christ, and although the deacon will conduct much of his triple ministry beyond the walls of church, he must never lose contact with the thread that connects him to the courts of the Lord.[*]

By "courts of the Lord," Fagerberg means the mysteries the deacon serves in the sanctuary of the church at Mass. This why all diaconal formation is, or should be, ordered toward the eradication of idolatry in the aspirant: He is being formed to proclaim salvation to the people from the ambo within the very rite announcing and communicating salvation from the one true God.

The celebration of the Paschal Mystery means to affect wor-

---

* David Fagerberg, *Liturgical Dogmatics: How Catholic Beliefs Flow from Liturgical Prayer* (Ignatius Press, 2021), 67.

shipers with eternal life. No man can be divided in such service. He must be a man of pure heart, one in possession of true knowledge of the true God. He must be a man who has surrendered his idols to the relationships that established his formation: confessors, spiritual directors, bishop, priests, theologians, God in prayer, the poor and the needy. In this surrendering, he might have noticed that his attachment to his favorite idols was deep, even too deep to give up without a fight or a bargaining posture toward God. "May I keep this escapist behavior in case of emergencies, in case I turn to you, God, in pain or desolation, and You do not immediately console me? May I?" It is very difficult to dismiss idols of immediate gratification. They attach themselves profoundly within the soul and may be even the last ones to leave a man.

But God is a jealous God and will not have rivals in our hearts (see Jos 24:19–20). In this way, He reveals himself as a nuptial God. He longs to give himself to His Bride, the Church, and He enables that one bride, through conversion, to give herself back to God and God alone.

The diaconal candidate's wife is also going through a conversion. Different dioceses require varying levels of participation for the wives of their deacon candidates, but minimally, the wife should be welcomed in some of the classes, be offered a spiritual director, be given designated wives' retreats, and have a counselor available to her to negotiate any disturbing or persistent emotional wounds in her life. One of the most powerful conversion experiences for many a wife is to witness and process her husband's conversion. It becomes a very moving meditation for her to enter. She watches her husband drop his idols and senses an invitation to identify her own. Now, the idols that attract her husband may not be the ones with which she struggles, but his victory in laying his down can inspire her to do the same with hers.

It can be most helpful for mutual conversion if the husband shares the graces of formation with his wife. What scriptural or theological truth most deeply affected his thinking in a new way? To what sin has he developed an aversion since formation began? What new spiritual attractions does he have as a result of the relationships he has entered into in formation? The husband can ask his wife if she has become aware of any new movements in her heart since formation commenced. Has she been made aware of any attractions in grace that are new to her? Are there any struggles that both husband and wife continue to wrestle with, either at the personal level or even at the doctrinal level, due to the classes they attend?

Some kind of processing between the spouses is helpful because of all that is being churned up within the heart as formation proceeds. Communicating about how formation is affecting daily life is a good way to internalize the work of the Holy Spirit. Many couples find such sharing of graces to be one of the most effective ways to protect the intimacy of their marriage. Instead of formation being "his" thing or a threat to the bond, such sharing can awaken the couple's gratitude to God over how formation is working to deepen their bond and wed them even more firmly to God in faith, hope, and love.

There are some diocesan formation processes that do not demand much involvement on the wife's part. On one level, this is good, as she is not the one being ordained. Her vocation is clearly that of a spouse and possibly a mother. Wives should have some latitude in discerning their level of involvement. After all, if a diocese demands too much participation in formation on the wife's part, it is almost surely choosing an elderly diaconate. Couples in their thirties should be able to freely discern how they will address the question of childcare during the formation process. I have seen many younger couples creatively negotiate the demands of formation with parenting in ways that truly served the formation process well. It is a shame for formators not to indicate that young couples are more than welcome in formation. It becomes an occasion for the deacon community to assist with arranging childcare, if needed. Creativity and flexibility around a wife's participation in formation is the best way to secure a younger demographic of future deacons.

Since men aspiring to the diaconate are at least in their thirties, it is common to think that formation has less effect upon them than those younger men in seminaries. This assumption is belied once formation leaders enter into discussion with the man's wife. In such conversations, the needed emotional and moral maturing of the man can be revealed. Chronological maturity alone may hide pockets of resistance to conversion, those idols again, from which formation wishes to set a man free. The United States Conference of Catholic Bishops' (USCCB) directory on diaconal formation expresses the need for this formation well: "The goal of a suitable human formation is to help the aspirant develop his human personality in such a way that it becomes a bridge and not an obstacle for others in their meeting with Jesus Christ."*

An aspirant to the diaconate should want to have grace root out of his heart any aspect of his personality that may lead others to avoid him and seek another for counsel or prayer. The whole movement of clerical formation invites a man to be generous in the work of any needed healing or conversion. To allow the Spirit to convert us from sin, mature us in affect, and commit us to deeper prayer is an act of charity toward the Church. A man may well summarize his time in formation in this way: "I am suffering moral change and spiritual growth so that my weaknesses do not turn others from seeking Christ." A man will want to be forthcoming in formation, inquiring of peers and formators how

* *National Directory for the Formation, Ministry, and Life of Permanent Deacons in the United States of America*, 2nd ed., 197.

his presence, actions, and habits are either winsome or unappealing. "Where do you see in me an area needing conversion, repentance, or healing?" This should be a common question candidates ask formators. The ideal candidate will be the one asking these questions of the formators and not one who waits for formators to "dig" into his heart. Self-revelation to appropriate formation leaders, peers, and always to God in prayer is the fastest way for a man to turn from his idols and live in reality.

How Aspects of Formation Influence Marriage

God calls married men into holy orders for several reasons:

- first, so the Church has proclaimers of the Gospel who, since they are in holy orders, can voice the very words of Christ amid the salvation being offered in the Mass
- second, so that flowing from this Eucharistic vocation, the Church may have ministers of consolation to those in need
- third, so that the man as deacon and the woman as wife can become saints
- fourth, so that the marriage bond may become more closely united with the Bridegroom Christ and His whole mysterious nuptial love toward the Church

In other words, God wants to deepen every good thing about marriage while simultaneously forming a new reality: a spousal deacon who publicly ministers out of his love for the mystery of Christ the Servant.*

Diaconal formation does not exist to make marriages stronger, but that is one of its results. The reason for this effect is clear:

* See James Keating, *The Heart of the Diaconate: Communion with the Servant Mysteries of Christ* (Paulist Press, 2015).

If a man comes to Christ in formation in order to let His servant mysteries[†] form him from within, it is inevitable that such conversion will make the man a better spouse. When one chooses to follow Christ more closely, He always improves his human character. If formation does not mature a husband's attentiveness to his wife, that may indicate a weak formation program or an anemic participation on the part of the husband candidate. One way a formation program can be weak is when it is reduced to "school" or "training" or the mere imparting of skill sets. This reduction is a betrayal of what the Church needs in her clergy. The formation program should be more akin to a few years of retreat, an *encounter with the living God* wrapped in intellectual reflection upon that encounter (the study of theology), and the equipping of candidates with needed competencies as *this divine encounter* calls a man into charity (liturgical and pastoral ministry). If formation yields no encounter with the Divine, then no formation for holy orders is occurring. If a program is facilitating an encounter with God but personal conversions are spare, then personal vulnerability may be its weak link. A man who simply wants to be a deacon but does not desire to be sent on mission from within a relationship with God reduces the vocation to its externals. Here, a man may be afraid of the conversion that follows from having intimacy with the Holy Trinity. He may fear getting too close to the fire of divine love in prayer. This is the fire that burns out one's affection for idols. Does this man want the flame to touch him? If he is not invited to excuse himself from formation, this man will retain his idols as he rises from the cathedral floor on ordination day. He will also remain an idol-enslaved husband bearing no maturation of character to his wife as gift.

Let us explore six aspects of formation that deepen a man's communion both with God and with his spouse.

† Mt 20:28; Jn 13:1–17; Mk 10:51–52; Lk 10:29ff.; 14:15–23; 17:7–10; 22:27.

1. Encountering the Living God: Conversion and Fidelity

One way to describe marriage is as a lifelong commitment in Christ to attain and remain in a loving communion of persons open to and at the service of life.* The married man seeking ordination should know that nothing within the vocation of holy orders undermines that commitment. The servant mysteries of Christ are those actions of Christ revealed in Scripture that embody His own self-donative mission. "What is most mysterious ... is precisely the infinite self-giving of God which is the fundamental characteristic of the divine Trinity and is enacted in history in the life, death and resurrection of Jesus."† A husband and wife participate in this self-giving within a sacramental marriage. They are ministers of Christ's own love and fidelity to one another. When lived in accord with the nature of diaconal prayer and ministry, a marriage can flourish in its reception of unforeseen graces. Such an integration of marriage and holy orders also aids in a spouse's capacity to be configured to Christ's cross as he or she experiences unforeseen sufferings. As both consoling graces and graces of suffering are shared in prayer to God and with one's spouse, the couple's emotional intimacy deepens. To enfold the diaconate within a life of loving communion between spouses is to layer and texture that marriage as a gifted adventure into holiness.

The optimum effect of a man entering the relationships that constitute diaconal formation is to receive anew his life with the living God. When done right, formation secures and internalizes a new level of engagement with God in prayer. This engagement is something the man wants to share with his wife. Depending on her participation in the formation processes, she may receive

---

* Perry J. Cahall, *The Mystery of Marriage: A Theology of the Body and the Sacrament* (Hillenbrand Books, 2016), 80–81.

† Mark McIntosh, *Mystical Theology: The Integrity of Spirituality and Theology* (Wiley-Blackwell, 1998), 44.

this engagement in the formation events along with her husband, or he may eagerly desire to share them with her upon his return home from formation. Either way, they should consider these questions carefully:

- Do you, as a couple, want to host God at a new level of Eucharistic worship?
- Do you want to engage God at a new level of intimacy through praying with the Scriptures (*lectio divina*)?
- Do you want to respond to such engagement by living a new freedom from idols?

In all sacramental formation, there is an aspect that attracts the heart ("Come, follow me" [Lk 18:22]) and an aspect that the heart resists ("Repent, and believe in the gospel, [Mk 1:15]). This *attraction and resistance* define the rhythm of formation. In this tension, we need to call upon the grace of God, His very life and love, both to continue attracting us into communion with Him and to communicate His strength so we no longer resist moral and spiritual conversion. Most frightening is our tendency to love our sins more than we love God. One reason we tend to choose sin over God is sin's pattern of delivering immediate gratification. God does not promise such gratification. Instead, He promises a sustained communion within ordinary affect. When one is addicted to immediacy, ordinary affect sounds "boring." God is not interested, however, in pandering to popular culture's addiction to immediacy. He wishes to free us from such habits and addictions so we might rest with Him. God is offering communion, not commotion.

The diaconal candidate and his wife should reflect on these questions:

- As a married couple, do you long for communion with one another, or do you sense a restlessness with your relationship?
- Are you looking for diversions? Distractions? Do you seek out what is new, novel, and next?
- Do you base much of your relationship on being entertained or entertaining new experiences?
- Can you be happy sitting in communion with your spouse? Can you sit quietly together in your home, or does that idea cause anxiety?

Encountering the living God in faith, hope, and love attracts. It has as its analogue falling in love. Encountering God is very much like being in the presence of the beauty of one's spouse. This beauty calls to us, invites us to come close, to reveal ourselves, and to trust its goodness. Both our spousal relationship and our spiritual relationship with God carry a call to find our peace within another person and not simply in events and experiences.

But hidden within beauty is yet another call. It is one that invites configuration. What God is giving is himself. He is holy. That which is not holy, that which God is not giving, must be surrendered, renounced. To live in His presence, we cannot take what He is not giving. What we have taken unjustly, like the fruit from the tree in the Garden, we must now surrender. This surrendering we resist. We struggle and suffer when we renounce sin because we grieve the loss of its emotional satisfaction. Clinging to this satisfaction, some turn from authentic formation in holy orders. If they continue in formation, they do so in a posture of "hiding" (Gn 3:8). They are not ready for communion; they possess a nostalgia for commotion.

To assist us both in following Christ and negotiating our resistances to such discipleship, the Church gives the deacon candidate formators, spiritual directors, confessors, and also his spouse. Within the deep and positive intimacy already attained within a mature marriage, deacon formation invites a further mission. It is the mission of renouncing any remaining idolatry in one's married life. Sin is all about isolation. Marriage and formation in holy orders are all about communion, relational prayer, intimate self-revelation, and choosing a love that communicates strength in one's battle to renounce sin. All clergy must suffer this renunciation of sin, as they must be the experts in leaving sin behind. How else can they describe the way of conversion to their parishioners if they have yet to suffer the same themselves? Identifying one's tendency to isolation from spouse and God is to identify points of idolatry. Isolation is different from solitude. Solitude is good and prepares a soul for deeper communion; isolation seals one off from communication with God or spouse so that the body, mind, or will can focus on selfish gain.

The worst thing a cleric can do is remain in sin and relativize its deadliness. Promoting relativism places the self at the center of one's thoughts and decisions. Instead, clerical formation places an encounter with the Holy Trinity at the center of all reality. This encounter with God is an encounter received as love, and such love carries one deeper into reality and away from the isolating tendencies of sin. Some dissenting clerics are captivated by placing the self and subjective experience at the center of their thinking. They promote this captivation by teaching and preaching that the doctrines defining sin are vestiges of past cultures, and they take the stance that, in today's culture, we have learned much from science and its constant discovery. Or they argue that cultural evolution through education has freed us from imposed truths; we now discover our own. What the Church teaches, especially in sexual ethics and medical ethics, simply limits her relevance. Such reasoning by dissenting clerics very often has self-interest at its core. Perhaps they love someone who holds or lives an ethic contrary to Church teaching. Or the deacon himself might continue to cling to a behavior he rationalizes as good or to an idea that fits with his commitment to a political party. This cleric wants to continue contracepting, masturbating, looking at pornography, supporting homosexual marriage, fostering openness to assisted suicide, allowing divorce and remarriage as a new cultural good, tolerating racial discrimination, promoting capital punishment, or the like. We naturally are attracted to the positive aspect of preaching, "God loves *you*." We all want to tell everyone that. Inside that news, however, is the cross. "Do you love God?" We have only one way to prove we love God: by our actions. These actions mentioned above are to be renounced as incompatible with being loved by God.

How difficult it is to be a public minister charged with preaching Christ crucified (1 Cor 1:23) and supporting the conversion of others as they mount their own crosses. No individual cleric is charged with updating the moral legacy of God's love. Only the Magisterium of the Church can discern what and how moral doctrine develops. It is vital that a man discern whether he wants to be a public minister preaching the cross and the Resurrection, not undermining it. It is the formation team's duty to see that only faithful men are ordained. "Proclaim the word; be persistent whether it is convenient or inconvenient; convince, reprimand, encourage through all patience and teaching. For the time will come when people will not tolerate sound doctrine but, following their own desires and insatiable curiosity, will accumulate teachers *and will stop listening to the truth and will be diverted to myths*" (2 Tm 4:2–4, emphasis added). Those who accommodate teachings to their own likings and resist authentic doctrine ought not to be ordained.

Whether it is a sin the candidate himself engages in or one his wife continues to practice, a deacon cannot promote dissent as a "development of doctrine." Advocating dissent from Church teaching cannot be a foundation upon which to build the process of clerical formation. Any man who is an advocate of such dissent should never be admitted to formation if his dissent is made known during the application process. If dissent is hidden from the diocese and comes to light during formation, it is simply a revelation of the man's own character. Such a revelation should initiate a discernment process on the question of his continuing in formation. Of course, struggling privately with habits of sin, renouncing them in confession, and knowing success and setbacks in overcoming temptation are all part of the normal journey into holiness. What appears as a serious obstacle to entering formation and remaining there would be one's personal dissent or public advocacy for change in moral doctrine. No one has a right to ordination, and it would be irrational to allow men into formation who have an agenda to undermine Church teaching. And yet such men are present in the ranks of deacons, preaching more as Democrats or Republicans, liberals or conservatives, than as Catholics.

If any man and his spouse are serious about pursuing a life of marriage and holy orders, they must first allow the living God to engage their consciences. Hiding doctrinal dissent from formators or the bishop under whom one is being formed is irrational or simply evil. The Church must have true knowledge of a man who desires holy orders so she can make informed decisions about accepting him into formation or continuing him in it. A man so desirous has an obligation to disclose any dissent for two reasons. First, he needs to make himself fully known to the Church so that, if he proceeds to ordination, he knows he has kept no secrets from his bishop. Only a man with no secrets should be ordained. A man is free only to the extent that his secrets are disclosed to the proper persons. Second, dissent is not only a confessional matter. For those in formation for holy orders, holding a dissenting position toward doctrine carries with it an obligation to disclose that position to the Church as represented by formators and spiritual directors. A man interested in a diaconal vocation must allow the fullness of attraction and resistance to the living God to find its end in receiving what God has given through His Church to be good and true. None of us is called to make our own truth and name it as good.

2. Living within the Living Word of God

Since marriage is the primordial sacrament,* meaning that it is the original sign in creation of how much God loves us, it remains a touchstone for us to remember our inherent dignity in the eyes of God. It is as if God is reminding us, "See how your spouse loves you and gives himself [or herself] to you as a gift; that is what I [God] do and intend to do for all eternity." This divine love reached its revelatory culmination in Christ's cross on Calvary. Here, the Bridegroom became complete gift, His complete self as the God-Man given over to the Father and, simultaneously, to humanity. By giving His body over to the Father and humanity in this way, Christ healed us from the scourge of death. Since He *is* the reconciliation of divinity and humanity, being one with Him in faith offers the hope of remaining alive with and in God after death. To secure such life in God, we have only to follow Christ, the One who has the "words of eternal life" (Jn 6:68). In Christ, in whom humanity and divinity are one, we have been given an invitation to align ourselves with Him and be carried into divinity (2 Pt 1:3–4), where we will safely exist for all eternity.

Marriage palely reflects this story of love that is God's creation and redemption. God is a seeker; He looks for His bride — each sinner — to invite that person into life and love. Men and women look for one another, and, finding the other, they rest in one another's presence within lifelong marriage. Such vowed presence mediates the healing of God and creates the condition for intima-

* John Paul II, *Man and Woman He Created Them: A Theology of the Body*, trans. Michael Waldstein (Pauline Books & Media, 2006), 19:4.

cy through self-revelation. It is this condition that enables a couple to attain a deep personal bond. Spiritual, emotional, and physical intimacy is the antidote to loneliness ("It is not good for the man to be alone" [Gn 2:18]). Marriage, as a communion of persons, embodies a sacramental sign that unveils God as the original communion of persons. God is that original, eternal communion, void of all loneliness and its evils. What we begin here on earth in marriage is completed and brought to perfection through Christ in heaven. There, we will participate in the eternal communion of love that is God.

This future realization is hinted at in the present through the promises of sacramentally married couples. By promising to remain together until death ("I am not going anywhere"), the couple's very life becomes a sign of God's fidelity to all of us. Pledging to remain together through grace in good times and bad, until death separates, enfleshes for the culture what God wishes to reveal about himself. Since we are sinners, we need to draw from God's love and life to make such an unconditional promise to our spouses. We know that suffering can tempt us to break promises and flee relationships. If we rely on our own weak wills, we are more likely to flee marriage when emotional suffering and economic or physical hardship arrives. Without the mystery of Christ internalized in us through worship, we are open to reducing our marriages to such times of suffering. In this way, suffering, rather than the relationship, becomes the couple's identity.

Here, we see that forgiveness is essential to a lifelong marriage. Gifting forgiveness to one's spouse is not a sign of failure or weakness but strength. Perfect marriages always include forgiveness as their essence. The Bridegroom himself taught us this from the cross as He asked the Father to forgive those who were making Him suffer. "Father, forgive them, they know not what they do" (Lk 23:34). As couples of faith, we are raised by grace to participate in Christ's own power of forgiveness and to bestow it upon our spouses throughout our married lives. Alone, we are not ordered toward such generous reconciliation, but in Christ, we share in His strength to do so. If we make it to our graves as married persons, we will have been touched by God's own life and love. That is how such a commitment, through sin and forgiveness, can endure.

Any couple who consider welcoming the diaconate into their marriage vows must have the life, death, and resurrection of Christ as their reservoir of vitality. Without Him as the foundation of the couple's spousal imagination, lifelong commitment can simply become a burden rather than a gift. The story of Christ *is* the story of marriage. His story must be what secures a couple's imagination. Living from that imagination, spouses can draw their own joy, faithfully navigating sufferings and losses. Having the life of Christ as the operating principle of one's imagination secures the possibility that, when difficulties arise, no other story but His will be the discerning rule of one's heart, thoughts, and will.

But first, Jesus' life, death, and resurrection must be internalized. How does His story become ours? How do we receive what we want Him to share with us? There are two simple entry points: participation in the Eucharist and the practice of *lectio divina*. There is one prerequisite commitment we need to make to secure such internalization: the renunciation of mortal sin. With such renunciation, both the bread of life and the word of God can penetrate freely into our hearts. When this condition is met, the internalization of the living Christ in our hearts will have its optimum effect. Renunciation of such sin must take place first in the Sacrament of Reconciliation. After this celebration of forgiveness and penance, one can begin to host Christ's own life to greater effect. To maintain such conversion from sin, we participate in the Eucharist and pray with Scripture. The more we do these acts of faith, the less we find sin attractive.

We do not root out sin on our own. Christ is at the heart of our battle to defeat sin. Remaining in relationship with Him is the victory we have over temptation. But Christ is also acting when we sense genuine guilt, express remorse, and know the grief of failing to turn from temptation. Such guilt is His call to us to return to real communion with Him. We want Him to be espoused to our hearts through our entire lives — and He wants that as well. He will see to it that we grow sick of sin, and He will see to it that we grow in delight with holiness. Our only duty is never to sever our lives from His — in good times or in bad, in suffering or in grace. One may say correctly that if we choose mortal sin, we have already divorced ourselves from Christ. This divorce, however, He does not will. He always remain close, calling, enabling, and securing our true conversions. He is the faithful spouse of our souls. Sin does not make God reject us; it makes Him come after us even more strongly. Sin does not repel God; it motivates Him. Remember, He comes looking for us: "Where are you?" (Gn 3:9). He knows we are always in the same hiding place. We always try to hide in sin. If we sin, we must let Him find us again. Eternal life depends upon our not remaining alone in sin, alone in our hiding place.

In the early stages of our marriage, my wife and I would engage in the practice of isolating ourselves after a fight. We would wrap ourselves in silence or make ourselves inaccessible by leaving each other's presence. One day, we were given a grace to stay in the same room after a disagreement. We sat there in our chairs. We picked up books to read. I was tempted to leave, but I stayed. She stayed. After a while, I forgot I was mad and said something. She responded. We ended the disagreement. Staying in each other's presence had a new feel to discovering an end to a disagreement. It symbolized that the pain we cause one another is not greater than the good of the communion within which we live. The communion must always triumph. I think this scenario reflects a little of what God intends. I think He stays in the room when we wander into our own pain and attempt to lessen it through sin. I think He is there sitting with us, allowing His presence to effect a change in our hearts.

So, as a man proceeds through diaconal formation, he should be encouraged to let God find him, to let his spouse find him, to fight to remain in communion. If we stray from communion, regaining it happens more quickly if we have the life and love of God internalized in our hearts. This internalization happens partially through the practice of *lectio divina,* through which we let Scripture feed our minds, concentrating God's life and love in our hearts so that our thinking will be the fruit of our love of God. As a result, we will begin our journey of becoming spiritual leaders. *Lectio* is the main way the truths of salvation reach our interior lives daily.

Lectio is prayerfully reading Scripture until we hear something; so the text should be brief, but the time we give to receive it in faith and silence should be substantial. During diaconal formation, a man is asked to study the Scriptures as an exercise in theology, in faith seeking understanding. Such study should never be alienated from prayer. Through faith, the Scriptures carry the presence of God into our hearts. Reading the Scriptures should lead us into prayer, into a loving rest with God. Such an approach to the Scriptures leads us to become contemplative. And what we contemplate orients us in spiritual leadership. As Pope Benedict XVI expressed it:

> However, knowing God is not enough. For a true encounter with him one must also love him. Knowledge must become love. The study of theology ... is not only knowledge of the propositions of the faith in their historical formulation and practical application, but is also always knowledge of them in faith, hope and charity. The Spirit alone searches the depths of God (cf. 1 Cor 2:10); thus, only in listening to the Spirit can one search

> the depths of the riches, wisdom and knowledge of God (cf. Rom 11:33). We listen to the Spirit in prayer, when the heart opens to contemplation of God's mystery which was revealed to us in Jesus Christ.*

Each day, time should be set aside for *lectio divina*. The following is one method:

- Approach the text in prayerful communion. Ask the Spirit to guide you through your reading and enlighten you about the meaning of concepts that quicken your affection for communion with God. No study will be completely irrelevant to you, as it will teach you truth and deepen your intimacy with Christ.
- Ask yourself: "What does this text say? What does this text say to me? What does this text lead me to say to God? What do I detect God is saying to me through this text?"
- Bring your contemplative insights before the Blessed Sacrament and let them rest there as your heart communes with Christ's Sacred Heart. Christ wants to deepen these insights in you because He wants you to be a man who thinks out of what he loves, and He wants you to love what is highest: himself.†
- Practice *lectio* with a spouse, thereby deepening communion both with her and with God. After silently praying with the text, the set of questions above can be shared with your spouse.

---

* Benedict XVI, Visit of the Holy Father to the Pontifical Gregorian University, (November 3, 2006), Vatican.va.

† I highly recommend the following books to deepen your sense of *lectio divina* and relational prayer: Jennifer Steffensmeier and Jessica Kary, AO, *Relational Prayer: A Small Group Guide* (Institute for Priestly Formation, 2023), especially page 96; Éamonn Bourke, *Make Your Home in Me: Reflections on Prayer* (Enroute Books, 2021).

3. Participating in the Self-Offering of Christ at Mass

For spouses to remain inspired by Christ the Bridegroom, who loved the Church and gave himself up for her (see Eph 5:25), a marriage needs a dynamic connection to the Eucharist. Each sacramental marriage is intrinsically linked to the Eucharist and so draws its spiritual nourishment from the spouses' participation in it daily or weekly, in their spending time with the Lord in Eucharistic adoration, and in their contemplating the mystery of Christ in Scripture. In having a connection to the Eucharist, the spouses choose to remain with Christ at the cross, that sign of complete spousal self-gift. Christ's crucifixion is the expression of His marriage to humanity and, at the same time, the origin and heart of the Eucharist.*

The purpose of the Eucharistic Liturgy is not to impart some data about God but to provide a personal encounter with Him. God wants to communicate himself to us. He does this in a way that humans can grasp, through the simple signs of bread and wine and the ministers in holy orders. The Eucharist is an exercise in spousal communication: God sees us in love; this leads Him to reveal himself and leads us to generously respond to Him; and that generous response leads us into sustained communion with Him. This is the process followed by all who fall in love and marry. In such a process between ourselves and our wives, or between God and each one of us, an encounter becomes internalized. God is seeking holy communion with us, and we are seeking the same with Him and with our spouses.

When a husband and wife reveal the truth about themselves to one another, they begin a journey into abundant life (Jn 10:10). Being vulnerable to the presence of one's spouse, a presence made more real by communication, is to be changed by that presence. It is to become what one is choosing to be: espoused in love.

---

* Benedict XVI, *The Eucharist* (USCCB, 2009), 50–51.

One reveals one's heart and responds in thanksgiving to what is revealed. Both marriage and the Eucharist involve a life-sharing communion of persons unto gratitude. Cultivating our consciousness regarding the real presence of our spouse is near the core of marriage in a way analogous to our surrendering to and acknowledging that Christ is truly present to us at Mass.

To lose consciousness of this spousal presence is to lose one's grasp of reality. But to acknowledge the presence of one's spouse as a gift contributes to our growth in vulnerability. In emotional and spiritual vulnerability, one is poised to host a presence, be it God or spouse. This presence affects and penetrates a person down to the source of his or her thoughts and desires. As a result of such vulnerability unto communion, the person begins to think like a spouse. Moving beyond bachelorhood, living no longer for himself, a man now thinks like one who is *in communion*. This is true also of the Catholic at Mass. One who worships moves out of the American cultural identity of independence, self-reliance, and privacy into a new liturgical "geography" that values self-revelation, communion, and mutual discernment.

To live in the presence of the spouse, however, is not to live in perpetual subjective satisfaction; suffering, boredom, and nonchalance (lack of interest) will be known. Imagining and wanting marriage to be a succession of self-satisfying events and, analogously, wanting Mass to be reduced to a forum of entertainment are regular temptations. But to critique marriage and worship according to the standards of entertainment is to stay entrapped in suffocating self-interest. The point of noticing the real presence of God or one's spouse is to be beguiled by the other's beauty. To choose to stay in the presence is to forget the self and slowly, developmentally enter communion. It is to attain a state of being akin to peace, not egocentric agitation. "Yet I live, no longer I, but Christ lives in me" (Gal 2:20). Some people do not like the Mass because it is the only hour of the week "not about *me.*" Some people do not like marriage for the same reason: It is not about me but about *my spouse.*

Both the Mass and marriage invite us to *die to self*, not to sustain both of those things by the life support of self-involvement. So the Mass and marriage establish us in a communion of presences. To sustain such communion, we are also bidden to sacrifice for it. At Mass, we are called to become assimilated into the very act of self-donation that is Christ's upon the cross. In doing this, we become capable, by grace, of suffering for the needs of our spouses, as Christ became capable of suffering for His. We are to lose ourselves in the action of Christ upon the Cross. "I surrender to You, Christ. Take me up *into Your kind of loving, the kind that only You can attain* for and within me." At Mass, we receive the love that is His in holy Communion and, thus, become able to sacrifice our lives for our spouses.

We need to share in Christ's life in order to love because "in the beginning" (Gn 1:1), instead of marrying God, we humans espoused ourselves to sin. Sin is the opposite of the Mass and of marriage: It is the refusal of self-gift and the use of reality to serve our own needs alone. It is the opposite of the generosity of the cross. To subvert sin, Jesus, as the God-Man, makes himself a gift.* Together, in marriage, a couple forms a new whole. The woman is the *helpmate in the things of God*, as we will see in chapter 3. Primarily, she reorients the man toward communion if his natural tendency to look outward and solve problems makes him veer away from his relations with God and others. And the man invites the woman to "see larger" when her identity is conflated with relations, when she is absorbed by them and loses her own sense of self.

Our greatest desire as spouses and persons is holy communion ("God alone satisfies" [CCC 1718]). It fulfills our need, our

* Michael Heintz, "An Encounter with the Word made Flesh: Louis Bouyer on Eucharistic Communion," *Gregorianum* 95, no. 4 (2014).

nature. We are relational beings. But our spouses cannot be the ultimate end of our desire for communion. We are created for *more* than our spouses: We are ordered toward an ultimate rest in God.

In the end, as in Christ's own life, our desires are meant to direct us to self-giving and receptivity in relation to spouse and God. This raises fears in us sometimes. "If I give myself away to God and spouse, who will give to me?" The mystery revealed by divine love addresses this fear. From revelation, we learn that the closer we come to God, the more we give ourselves — the more, in fact, we become ourselves. We enter a mutual reciprocity of self-donation flowing from the source of love itself, the Holy Trinity.

In worshiping God, we are called to contemplate Him (in the actions and person of Christ) and empty ourselves of idols. In "worship" of our spouses, we are called to behold them and empty ourselves of those selfish distractions that prevent us from remaining in their real presence. In the Eucharist, our deepest desire to be loved by God receives a confirmation that such rest will be given eternally. In the Eucharist, we receive a second sign that our hope for love will not be extinguished at death. That sign is the history of one's own spousal love. From such a history, it is reasonable to believe that such love, albeit not in marriage itself, will not be lost in eternal life but is secured in Christ. Life and love go on. Being *in Christ* — that is, being assimilated into His saving actions through the sacramental life and the theological virtues — men and women live in hope of eternal joy together as espoused to God.

In worship, we come to know a deepened gratitude for our spouses and learn to hold their presence lightly (not absolutely), as death will usher husbands into the *Source* (God) of their spouses' life and beauty. Our spouses are not the Source; rather, our spouses reflect the Source's desire for us, God's own desire to marry humanity. Both wife and husband experience a glimpse into this tension — into a spouse's being the *reflection* of beauty, not its *source* — when, as a deacon, the husband leaves the side of his wife (relative good, reflection) to enter the sanctuary (heaven, source). Catholic marriage is a journey of purification and gratitude, conversion and worship. The spouses prepare one another to accept that God is all in all. He alone penetrates the heart and, thus, that heart survives death, living on in the very source of married love. This mystery of endless love is encountered and secured in the Mass. Each spouse is taken up into the very spousal self-giving of the Bridegroom, Christ, toward His Bride, the members of the Church.

As spouses and Christians, we are called to a life of bodily self-surrender in response to the bodily self-surrender of God himself toward us. As God and man were one in Christ's body, we, as humans, now have hope to live a similar life, a human life infused with divine life. Christ wants to give us this: "I have been crucified with Christ, yet I live, no longer I, but Christ lives in me; insofar as I now live in the flesh, I live by faith in the Son of God who has loved me and given himself up for me" (Gal 2:19b–20).

We need to give ourselves to Christ through our gift of self to our spouses (sacrament), the poor (mission), and God himself upon the altar (worship). In turn, God will *continue* to give us all we have ever desired but that has taken a life's journey to believe: "All I have ever wanted was *You*."

4. Meeting One's Own Poverty in Serving Others

The sacrifice that the Mass and marriage call us to make is a moral requirement. Remaining in communion with spouse and God is a sacrifice because our first inclination is to provide for the self rather than serve spouse and worship God. We need to be formed by moral truth, as a core component of being in relation to Christ, so that His grace can bend us away from such natural self-involvement. We have a predilection toward self-interest. At first, we love pleasing the self as our priority; but as we mature in the ways of discipleship (human development), we come to realize that satisfying the self as our prime concern is a suffocating experience. We must learn the real joy known by saints and lovers. This joy is found in acknowledging our inability to leave selfishness completely behind. To move beyond selfishness, we need divine assistance; we need to ask for the graces of self-forgetfulness. Being in communion with Christ gives us the hope that such forgetfulness is possible. Here, we experience our own poverty. We are not self-sufficient. We cannot will ourselves out of our fallen state, our penchant for sin. This recognition becomes a gift. Our powerlessness to do the loving thing invites us to deepen our communion with Christ. To think of others' needs, we must participate in Christ's own love. Discipleship is remaining poor and dependent on God's life and love. Although we are poor, we are rich now in relatedness to God.

Moreover, from our own poverty, we are invited to have empathy toward the weakness of others. Christ empowers us to become agents of hospitality by participating in His own generous heart through worship. During formation, the deacon candidate will be asked to host many new acts of charity in his heart. Formation will stretch the candidate and test whether he can relinquish his former ways of "mastering" a task or achieving or managing or working toward goals alone. Can he, instead, remain vulnerable to grace and let Christ live His own love over again in the candidate's body?

Of course, if the candidate is married, hosting love and learning sacrifice will not be completely new. If he is a father, he knows the sacrifice of child-rearing and the spousal sacrifices he offers for his wife. But formation is moving a man more deeply into society and beyond the familiar features of spousal love. Diaconal ministry opens a man to the commitment to love neighbor and stranger in the name of the Church. He will learn to engage in charity as a public person, as a cleric in the Church and not simply as a kind and charitable citizen. Ministry is dependency on Christ. It is His service that the deacon renders, and so ministry's purpose is better served if the deacon remains in a posture of prayer. The deacon is called to receive even while giving. Analogically, it is like a husband's gaining strength and consolation from his wife's loving presence as he faces another day of challenge or weariness at his work or profession. Being in communion with her gives him the energy to face his commitment to serve the greater good of the family in his work. Christ, too, internalized through faith, communicates strength and effectiveness to the deacon as he visits the sick, counsels a grieving spouse, or instructs a resistant parishioner.

Formation will not work for those men who cannot embrace the fact that they are being called into a supernatural service. Ministry is not drawing from one's native talents to achieve a purpose. One approaches ministry as a beggar of grace. Those who insist on reducing religion to ethics, to a simple humanism, miss the entire point of ordination. One is ordained *because* ministry is *not* the man's; it is God's. Ministry is not mastering skill sets. Ministry is this: "He must increase; I must decrease" (Jn 3:30). This poverty also belongs to the candidate's spouse. She must be willing to yield to a new supernatural force within her marriage. This power of the person of Christ invites her to a new level of trust and a new participation in faith as well. She, too, becomes more of a public person as her husband's service exposes him to the congregation more visibly. She, too, must learn to depend on Christ to help her discern new ways of being espoused to her husband, accept new demands upon the family, and be open to new graces and challenges to process and internalize.

As formation continues, the candidate's marriage itself tastes a certain poverty. In hosting public ministry as a new part of spousal love, many of the former coping mechanisms and strategies to remain connected as a couple may have to yield to longer, deeper prayer, counsel from experienced clerics, and creativity in considering new schedules and routines. There will be the need to surrender more to Christ as He continues to move deeply in places familiar to a sacramental marriage; but now, He approaches anew. Christ now approaches the couple not simply as the Divine Spouse aiding their marital love but as the Divine Servant inviting the deacon into His own ministry, and the deacon's wife into a service of her own. Her service is to remain in the gaze of Christ, receiving His gratitude for any sacrifices she makes so that Christ's own diaconal ministry can flourish.

This new aspect of the couple's relation to Christ most directly affects the husband; he is the one carrying the mission of the Envoy-Servant Christ, but the wife is challenged as well, invited to let grace possess her husband through her cooperative and generous heart. She will, at times, experience her own poverty in the face of her husband's commitment to serve. The wife needs to remain in continual communication with God in prayer and with her spouse in conversation. In this way, she avoids the temptation to lose her identity in her husband's new vocation or resist his mission by pretending something new has not entered their marriage. To lose her identity is not her new vocation. Nor does ignoring the diaconate preserve her identity in any real way. The integration of this new aspect of her husband's life into her love for him is the only healthy way both to preserve her identity and to offer to celebrate his. Alternately, the deacon husband must welcome holy orders into his body in a way that deepens his own awareness of the presence and needs of his wife. As one configured to the Envoy-Servant Christ, the deacon husband offers his own poverty to Christ to be filled with divine generosity in the mission of spousal love and ecclesial service.

5. Committing Oneself to Interior Living

All this hosting of the supernatural is an invitation to a deeper, more dynamic prayer life. Becoming a cleric and addressing the state of one's spiritual life are coextensive. Some deacon formation programs fail to address the importance of forming deacons as contemplatives. Yet this is a vital aspect of the vocation for two reasons: First, the deacon is a proclaimer and preacher of the living word of God. This mystery, Christ becoming Incarnate, must be internalized in the deacon's heart so that when he preaches, he does so out of the communion he has with God and within which he lives. Second, there is an often muted reality within the diaconate that must become more conscious within the minds of all in formation. Each deacon must ready himself for the celibate life. If a deacon's wife predeceases him, then the Church requires the deacon to remain celibate. Since this aspect of the clerical life is often overlooked in formation, there have been some sad situations in many dioceses where men have left the diaconate to marry again after losing their wives to death.

A man dedicated to contemplation is a man dedicated to beholding the beauty of God in love through prayer. To contemplate is to allow the mind and soul to rest in God as love and lover. All true celibates are contemplatives because it is only in contemplative prayer that the erotic needs of a man can find fulfillment. The erotic is simply that aspect of being human that seeks out another, someone beyond the self, with whom one can give love and receive love. Normally this is done in marriage. But even in marriage, the spouse is not the ultimate person in whom the human heart rests. That ultimate Person, God, is always searching for us. He desires to share His life and love with us so that we might respond in kind. Our spouses reflect the love of God, Christ loving His Bride; but together, the spouses must rest only in God as their ultimate and eternal love. If the deacon does not seek out God in contemplative prayer, he is poorly prepared to preach, teach, counsel, and pray with others. And he is poorly prepared for a celibate life if his wife should die before him.

During formation, a husband and wife should seek out times to enter into contemplative silence together and individually. This kind of prayer can be done in concert with *lectio divina* to reach its true purpose in the silencing in one's heart of all the noise present in popular culture. From within this silence, one can better internalize the love of God. It is praiseworthy to reflect upon God's love and allow its beauty to silence us during our time in praying with Scripture or in Eucharistic adoration. All deacons should strive to practice at least one Eucharistic devotion a day, either assisting at daily Mass or praying for some time before the Blessed Sacrament. As one's interior life becomes more and more silent, and the distractions that pass through our minds from contemporary culture are replaced with a stable Christological imagination, one matures in contemplation.

The prayer life of a man in formation grows as he incorporates into his daily routine the advice of his assigned spiritual director. It is very helpful if the spouse of the deacon-aspirant also engages a spiritual director. She needs a director so that her spousal identity in Christ can rise to all the challenges of being married to a cleric. She can also benefit from direction in order to internalize all the graces that are given to her in her own personal prayer. It will be spiritually wise to continue to talk to a spiritual director on a regular basis after ordination. Satan wants to disrupt the life and ministry of deacons, as well as to mischievously divide the deacon and his wife in the spousal union. Having a director to talk to about one's commitment to prayer and vocation can be very fruitful over the duration of clerical life.

6. Leaving the American Way of Life and Entering the Liturgy as One's New Native Land

The last feature that a husband and wife will want to discuss together during the formation process is any call from the Spirit to relate differently to "this age" (Rm 12:2). As noted in previous chapters, the American popular and political culture is a strong agent of our imagination's formation. It rivals what the Church can form in us, as its messaging and images are relentless across many forums in daily life, whereas the Church usually gets an hour on Sunday. For many — perhaps most — deacons, the secular culture was their dominant formator before they began diaconal formation. The popular culture has been most men's tutor since adolescence and even before, depending upon the emotional and spiritual health of their family.

When I use the term *popular culture*, I mean those aspects of the Western value system that promote immediate gratification; materialism; obsession with youth, beauty, health, and relaxation; travel as escapism; and various cyberspace distractions and social media. Of course, the culture as a whole is wider than these questionable attributes and behaviors. It also includes statesmanship, worship, music, the arts, sports, economic growth, family, labor, care for the earth, and other positive realities. Despite a culture's challenges, one cannot simply critique culture; one also must behold the beauty of what humans create and value. As Cardinal Francis George wrote: "A culture is transformed only by those who love it, just as individuals are converted only by evangelizers who love them. … The best way to evangelize is through witness and the practice of holiness. … The saints will always ratify what is best about a culture, they will always properly critique what is demonic about it."*

While cultures influence us, they do not determine our identity. We are free to rise above them, critique them, and move to reorient them in light of a greater truth: that God wants to form humanity. Diaconal formation should be a set of relation-

* Francis Cardinal George, OMI, *The Difference God Makes: A Catholic Vision of Faith, Communion, and Culture* (Crossroad, 2009), 58.

ships that purifies a man's heart and reorders it toward authentic worship of the Holy Trinity. This kind of formation moves the man to heal any ideological thinking in him that is sourced in partisan politics or philosophies antithetical to an authentic Catholic anthropology. A cleric's understanding of human life, morality, and social interaction emerges from worship. From worship, one's reason and affect are healed and elevated, and this aids the person in discerning what thoughts and behaviors originate in expedient pragmatism. In such a case, the will and the mind have been tutored by only partial goods and incomplete truths. A mind that inhabits worship as its source for truth will not rest in only the pragmatic; it wants to receive truth itself. Jesus, who takes us to the Father in the Spirit through Eucharistic participation, *is* the Truth (Jn 14:6). It is He who needs to form our minds and hearts, not "this age."

As a man and his spouse become vulnerable to the content of clerical formation, they will find a new freedom, a new detachment from the values that make up popular culture. Over time, formation will assist a man in securing his identity more deeply to the things that do not change. A man can be a herald of the Good News only if he has discerned correctly which sources in culture are compatible with that proclamation and which may undermine it. As a result of formation, a cleric becomes a man of discernment. This is one of his great gifts that he brings to his parish, his neighborhood, and his circle of friends.

To be a man of discernment is to be one who listens for the voice of God as the *last word* and becomes adept at noticing what is simply the *latest word* carried through the popular culture. He is a man fastened to truth and not to superficial emotions or trends or fashions of any kind. The cleric clings to the living word of God as it reveals itself, streaming its grace from the altar, the ambo, and the teaching of the Church. The man of discernment attends to the lives of the saints as sources of behavioral and dispositional modeling. The discerning cleric hears what is passing through culture so that he can measure it against what he is listening to in worship and ecclesial life. Such a man knows the stream of truth that carries humanity deeper into dignity and knows the things that undermine that dignity, pandering only to those aspects of humanity that respond to self-involvement.

For a deacon to be in the popular culture but not of it means that he must eschew partisan ideology, resist immediate gratification, be painfully reoriented by true worship, and find freedom in the intellect by binding it to doctrine. Becoming a Catholic man, now configured to the diaconal aspect of Christ's identity, may be the most difficult conversion one undergoes. The wife of such a man must share in these changes as well. Even though the conversion is not hers specifically, she obviously will know its effects in the marriage. Such a conversion is especially difficult if the couple are essentially Americans who worship rather than worshipers who happen to be Americans.

If the couple are not receiving quality spiritual direction and are without access to psychological counseling within formation, this conversion from being citizens of the popular American culture as the generator of identity to becoming inhabitants of the Eucharist as the generator of identity might threaten spousal unity. The presence of such disunity makes sense if what linked the couple together was not the quest for holiness but, rather, a shared interest in the superficial activities of culture. In this case, religion was only an added dimension of life and not the true culture upon which their lives together were founded. What formation is asking of a couple is to brace themselves to move from one "place of residence" to another. This new place of residence is one that is the fulfillment of all the sacraments of initiation and the Sacrament of Matrimony. This new place of residence, one that American popular culture cannot co-opt, presents itself as both inviting and frightening. In order for the couple to live there, God provides His grace and gives the couple new companions on the way. But the transition may be disturbing. Of course, one could become a deacon and remain a citizen of popular culture, but what kind of complex form of life would that be? Why would one subject spouse and family to that kind of complexity and stress, when an authentic vocation is one of simplicity and inner peace? Such simplicity and inner peace are awarded to those who truly enter formation and end up "residing" in the Liturgy. It is the responsibility of the formation process to really want its men to make this move.

CHAPTER 3

Marriage Ordered Toward the Holy: Daily Life

When formation is faithful to its own purposes, more likely than not it gifts a wife with a more morally attractive and better-suited husband than the one she first encountered at the altar on her wedding day. If his transition from being a citizen of popular culture to being a citizen of worship has been successful, many of his immoral aspects, and even some emotional wounds, have been healed. He is a man who knows Christ more intimately, more deeply, than before formation began. He is a man who holds all but his vocation as spouse, father, and deacon more lightly; and as a result, he is a simpler man, a free man, and one a wife can live with more easily — "easily" in the sense that the husband's conversion has made his heart more accessible in communication, and therefore, the spouses have become more united. Complex men, diffused in their identity and behaviors, make difficult spouses. Simple men are ones who are self-possessed because they have become possessed by Christ. They no longer seek to please others, seek their approval, or need their acceptance to grasp their self-worth and meaning. The simple man, the ordained man, the self-possessed man has become such because he has suffered the death of his ego in formation, has renounced the idols of culture, and has established himself as free through citizenship within the Eucharist. Such a citizen lives free in the popular culture because he is attached to the supernatural at the altar. This altar he now humbly assists at as deacon.

Daily life with such a man is better emotionally for the wife, but it is still ordinary. Participating in a quality formation program to become a deacon is life altering, but it is still a human life a deacon leads. A wife will notice changes in her husband, but she will also notice that some stubborn "thorns" in the side remain, or at least have not been fully removed by grace (see Nm 33:55). Rejoicing in the newness of her husband, she may also have to call upon her own reserves of courage, patience, and grace to abide with his backsliding or even his own ministerial insecurities after ordination. Living as a native of the Eucharist in the diaconate will involve much gratitude from both spouses, but it is still a journey *into* holiness that defines both the marriage and holy orders. Satan hates both marriage and holy orders and will actively try to undermine the marital union and the confidence to minister that now defines the husband's life.

After formation is complete and ordained life begins, there will be the tension between the "already" and the "not yet." That is the tension of having undergone conversion but remaining vulnerable to thinking that life back in the popular culture (or "Egypt" [Ex 16:3]) has its merits. Satan will play on that tension and often tempt a couple to "move back to America" and only *visit* the land of the Eucharist. Remaining natives of the Eucharist will be the goal in this spiritual tug-of-war.

It is important to remember that the spiritual life can easily be dismissed and forgotten. Since we worship a God who is pure spirit, it takes a dedicated commitment to prayer each day in order to remember and remain in His presence. The Incarnation was God's greatest gift to us for many substantial reasons, but one aspect of this gift is clear: We now have a human life to contemplate that assists us in internalizing the holy and transcendent God. As mentioned above, the practice of daily *lectio divina*, the Liturgy of the Hours, Eucharistic devotion or assistance at Mass, and shared prayer between spouses will go a long way to keep alive and deepen a deacon's intimacy with God.

A deacon must guard and protect his spiritual life so that Satan does not rob him of his devotion. To speak to and attempt to listen to the Spirit can be a difficult life's commitment, especially when that Spirit is sovereign and knows exactly what level of affective response during prayer is best for us. Prayer is *not* an endless stream of consoling feelings. The movement away from the idolatry of immediate gratification will be a regular battle in prayer, a battle tempting us to minimize our prayer time or eschew it altogether. Since prayer is a normally private form of communication and no one knows if we are praying or not, Satan likes to attack our prayer commitment, tempting us to forsake it. After all, other than God, who knows that you have given up prayer? Oftentimes, only yourself.

Here is where a spouse can be a particular gift to the deacon. It is a good practice for a husband to explicitly invite his wife to encourage him to go to the church and adore the Lord or to assist at Mass. She may also be a great partner in battling Satan when she joins her husband in morning or evening prayer. In spiritual and emotional maturity, the deacon is solely responsible to see to his own relationship with God. However, as Eve was Adam's helpmate in the things of God, so all wives can be for their husbands. It is important to know that *helpmate* in the book of Genesis refers to something very specific in the relationship a woman has to her husband. The Bible uses the word *helper*[*] (*ezer* in Hebrew) to refer to Eve, but this same word is frequently used for God himself (e.g., Ps 54:6). The woman is the man's helper because she assists him in fulfilling the deepest purpose of his life: to give himself to God. Both spouses help one another come to see God as their ultimate love.

The woman has a more innate sense of guarding and promoting the communion of relationships. By our nature, as made in the image and likeness of God, we know communion with others to be our very peace. It is not good to be lonely, emotionally isolated, or self-sustained in any way. God is a communion of Persons, and so, since we are made in His image, we thrive when loneliness or alienation has been overcome in favor of relations with others and with God. A wife can be a real gift to a deacon in inviting him to remember that remaining in communion with God each day is his deepest vocation.

The Diaconal Duties: Threat or Gift to Domestic Routine?

No doubt, becoming a deacon is adding another commitment to an already full life of marriage and raising children. However, I would encourage any man who is a father of young children *not* to put off entering formation and seeking ordination simply because of his paternal status. There is a "rule" held by many pastors, deacon formators, and bishops that one should not integrate diaconate into a marriage where young children are present. Thinking it charitable for such a father to be denied entry into formation, some formators insist that a man wait until

[*] Mary Healy, "St. Paul, Ephesians 5 and Same-Sex Marriage," *Catholic Culture*, https://www.catholicculture.org/culture/library/view.cfm?id=9790.

his children are at least in high school. This is one of the circumstances that has inadvertently turned the diaconate into a "retirement" vocation. Pastoral leaders of goodwill have rejected younger men pursuing a vocation.

I have known many men in their thirties and forties who became ordained and successfully integrated fatherhood into the diaconal way of life. Of course, one must have a spouse who wishes to suffer such a vocation with her husband. There will have to be compromises, new priorities, and new scheduling. Some avocations may have to be delayed, rather than delaying the vocation. This is most vital for men to consider if they have younger children in the household: Will you be able to do as little ministry as possible?

A common disposition among newly ordained ministers is that the Church expects them to do a lot of work. Some new deacons think they must practically live on the parish grounds. This is an error. If such a life is communicated to you by your pastor, he is misguided. The diaconal vocation is not sacrificial in the way the priestly vocation is, where a man gives his entire life to pastoral presence. Nor is ordination about feeding the American disease of workaholism. A deacon discerns which ministries he can accept according to their integration into spousal and paternal love, as well as professional responsibilities. No deacon ministries should look alike, and no deacon should ever compare his own ministry with that of other deacons in some judgmental fashion. Ministry is not a contest to be won, measured by the clock. It is a presence to be shared within the context of each man's unique circumstances. A deacon makes himself available to God to discern what mission can best be integrated into fatherhood and spousal love. Workaholism kills relationships, even the one with God. Workaholism is a misplaced belief that you are "needed everywhere." This can be attached to the idol that I mentioned earlier: worshiping the goal of winning approval.

The greatest threat to a married clergy is the festering of unhealed emotional wounds in a husband (insecurity, anxiety, self-loathing, perfectionism, people pleasing, etc.). These wounds cry out for healing but seek a balm that can itself exacerbate the wound. This ineffective balm bids the deacon try harder, work a lot, confuse unhealed neediness for generous availability, and minister as one seeking approval or admiration or to become irreplaceable. Unlike priests who live celibate lives of unfettered availability to God and practice uniquely *necessary ministries*, deacons are fettered to family and profession and practice *a useful and spiritually enriching ministry*, not an urgent or necessary one. Who has ever cried out for a deacon on his or her deathbed? When a man has offered these and other emotional wounds to the proper agents of healing during formation, he begins to possess a mature freedom about which ministries to enter and which ones to refrain from accepting. Busyness is not equivalent to acts of love. The one who is loved rests in the love received and given. Such receptivity frees a man from calculating whether he is "winning" or "better" or "needed" more than others. God does not need us. God's presence in us wishes to be received by us so that this presence might overflow onto others. Ministry is letting the One who loves you affect the needs of those to whom you are present. Ministry is not an effort to get God's attention; it is an effect of remaining in his presence and being vulnerable to his love.

It is common to confuse workaholism with generosity. But workaholism or ministering out of neediness or to gain proof of one's worth is the opposite of generosity. Generosity generates life. Workaholism or functionalism, seeking our identity in what we do, robs us of life. The difference between a workaholic and a hard worker is that the one who works hard is free to leave his duties, even reduce them, to strengthen and maintain his emotional ties with his family and God, whereas a workaholic severs those ties in the name of "obedience" or "fidelity." This is a trap.

Unfortunately, some wives see their husband's new clerical vocation through the lens of "gifting him" to the Church. Under this disposition, she can, at times, "suffer in silence." What is the suffering? She knows that the ministry in which her husband is engaged is threatening their bond, but because it is "holy" work and work "for God," she is reluctant to speak the truth: The diaconate is not weakening the marriage, but her husband's unhealed wounds are.

Diaconal duties can be integrated into marriage, even marriages with small children, if the deacon sees communication with his wife as a priority, is committed to discerning prayer with God daily, and prudently uses the word *no* when more and more demands pile up from pastoral needs. As deacons, we are not needed everywhere, just somewhere. Considering diocesan realities, pick that place and stay fastened to its humble parameters. Looking for more to do may be a sign not of one's virtue but of a lack of virtue. Christ never quantified that we must do a lot of activity; He simply invited us to share in His own.

Spousal Communication: Sharing Prayer, Feelings, New Decisions

When a wife senses that the bond of intimacy, born of sharing affective movements of the heart, is in peril, the Church hopes she will find her voice to protect that bond. A wife recognizes that a pastor needs help, but she also recognizes that he does not need the help of just one man (her husband). Discernment teaches that lay ministers can assist the pastor with the burdens he carries just as well as a fellow cleric. What exactly does a pastor need a deacon to do? The short answer is that particular ministry that is best suited to the man's natural gifts and the charisms born of ordination. Obviously, this means sacramental ministry and preaching, as well the exercise of the grace of ordination as it extends Christ's blessings and healings in prayer with and counsel to parishioners. One hopes that more pastors will request deacons from their bishops so they can have brother clerics to pray with and envision parochial ministry with in order to execute that vision together. A deacon is not simply "help"; he is a spiritual brother to priests and a spiritual leader in service to the laity. But, of course, the deacon must be formed as such, and seminaries must define the deacon as someone more than simply a functionary whom a priest can use when he is too busy to go to the nursing home or preside at a vigil service.

During formation, an aspirant and his wife must confront threats to their intimacy head-on. The wounds leading to workaholism lead a new deacon to unknowingly cooperate with a priest's own unhealed wounds of laziness or authoritarianism or prejudice against the diaconal state. The new deacon and his wife want to serve, but they want to do it within the confines of the life into which God has called them. Only if a wife and her deacon husband are faithful to the integrated life given them as their vocation will sanctity be theirs. At times, in the name of becoming saints, a deacon and his wife must refuse to expand their already full life of love and service. The pastor will have to understand. Most will, unless a pastor, too, persists in his unhealed wounds. We are all wounded healers, but the wounds borne by such healers refer to the limits of human nature, not those wounds that could be healed through therapy and pharmacology. For these to be healed, they must be revealed. When not revealed, these recoverable wounds tend to spread their pain to others as well. In choosing not to be healed ourselves, we make all those around us suffer as well.

Whenever a deacon comes up with a new idea for ministry, he should take it first to silent prayer and welcome the fullness of God and the wisdom such listening brings. Afterward, he should propose it to his wife, and they should enter a conversation about vocational fidelity together. No speaking is authentic unless it has first been born in the silence of listening to God and the truth of one's circumstances. From such silence, the spouses' conversation with each other can be generated. For a married couple, the only end of such a conversation is to discern whether this new ministry can be integrated into the intimacy they have already achieved and wish to deepen. If not, it should be rejected. It cannot be conducive to growth in holiness. Ministry should not weaken the marriage into which it has been welcomed.

Attending to Your Sons' and Daughters' Experience of Becoming Public Persons

In the excitement of entering a new vocation, with new commitments lying ahead, parents may neglect to check with the children on how they are experiencing their dad's new vocation. How have the responsibilities of diaconal formation and ministry affected their sense of purpose and emotional security? A father does not have to get "permission" from his children to pursue formation as a deacon, but he does have to listen to their input. This is especially true to help in discerning what time might be best for the family to enter formation. Once their father is accepted into the formation process, the children should be asked to share its impact on their sense of family unity, personal happiness, and the effects it has had on their shared time with Dad and Mom.

Some of the demands of formation cannot be adjusted to address the needs of children. If the mother and father see that formation is negatively impacting the children in a substantial way, then the only recourse is to adjust the habits and schedules of home life. The entry of a father into the deacon program ought not make the family unduly sacrifice or suffer. The one who is called to sacrifice in both the service of formation and family unity is the father. The preponderance of sacrifice should be on his shoulders. He should be the one to change the most, reducing time on television or computer or phone to be present to his children. It is he who must minimize his time spent doing hobbies, watching sports, or playing games. He may have to, where possible, adjust work time when it is deemed excessive.

Having a father become a public person is not always a smooth transition for children. In some cases, a deacon's children undergo teasing or forms of mild emotional abuse from peers. This is especially true if the children attend the parish school at which their deacon father is assigned. Children in schools outside the parish may not even know what a deacon is or if any peers are children of a deacon. But for those children who see their classmates at Sunday Mass, and they, in turn, see their friend's dad in vestments and preaching, some singling out has been known to happen. "Are you going to be a *priest*, too, Tommy?" "Now you have to be holy, Tommy, just like your dad." And so on. Checking in with the children regularly and explicitly about how this topic is being treated by peers is the best way to uncover such teasing and address it appropriately.

Entering the vocation of a deacon can also lead to surprising experiences for a family, including the possibility of new friends. Many deacons have introduced their children to one another in the diocese, leading to new and close friendships for the children. Being welcomed more deeply into the deacon community can assist children to be less self-conscious about their unique social status.

Loss of Social Life

It is rare that a vocation to the diaconate will weaken ties with longtime friends. But certainly, one's friendship circle might not expand after ordination; some people will be uneasy having clergy at parties or other gatherings. On the other hand, of course, one may find new friends through the formation process itself.

This is a true gift. Such friendship, however, is not always certain, as there are many circumstances that make "staying in touch" after ordination a difficulty not easily overcome. But real, lasting friendships with other deacons and their wives add to the quality and joy of having received such a vocation.

It can happen, however, that some in the parish or diocese may refrain from including the new deacon in their house parties or barbecues or dinner dates because, well, "he is different now." One may argue that the new deacon is not "different," and even that he has become more himself since ordination, but such a plea may not be heard. Any such rejection by peers at the adult level is usually an irrational action based upon the peers' immature grasp of what faith, religion, and holiness really entail. Such fellow parishioners may also be less keen about having clergy at their summer gatherings or sports viewing parties, thinking the deacon would be uncomfortable. The casualty of a diminishing social life is not the greatest suffering post ordination, but it can be real. This can often affect the spouse even more, as she was not expecting such collateral damage to her social life because of her husband's entering the clergy.

The Relationship Between Work and Evangelization

There is continuity between the person one was before ordination and the person one is after. Formation does not invite a man into *a role* to be played like an actor but into a *receptive posture toward Christ.* Throughout formation and beyond, the Church invites the deacon to do the sometimes hard work of staying in love with God. This love is making him a new creation. The change is happening organically within his own personality and habits. What is this change? It is the deepening of his love for the Most Holy Trinity, as this love configures him uniquely to Christ. This configuration is diaconal in that Christ is asking the man to let Him live His own envoy-servant mysteries over again in his body. If he has cooperated with formation generously and freely, the personality he has will become more attractive to others, not less. Being in love with God and receiving configuration to Christ's servant mysteries as one's vocation is something that births joy in a man. This joy will be a winsome aspect now present in a more mature and integrated personality.

Each man must decide for himself how to reveal his new vocation to his work colleagues. How should this be done? When should it be done? Should it be done explicitly or only episodically when the need arises on the job? How and when should one's status as a clergyman be revealed? Should one announce to colleagues that he is in formation, or should he wait until an ordination date has been given to him? When should a conversation be had with bosses or managers, as formation may affect work schedules? All these questions and more are best explored with one's wife, pastor, and other men already ordained. They can assist a candidate in weighing what is best for the man in formation, his career, and his family.

During formation and once ordained, how should a deacon negotiate the public nature of his religious commitment? American culture does not normally welcome overt evangelizers in the workplace. And yet, God embeds deacons as ambassadors of the Eucharist in that environment. In doing so, one would think that He wills a man to extend the Good News to professional colleagues. The question is not "Should I?" but "How do I?" Of course, circumstances vary widely in each person's workplace. One work environment may welcome hosting Bible studies, while others clearly communicate that religion is a "private" matter and is not to be discussed during the eight-hour workday. There have been legal cases adjudicated over workplace hostility toward religion. There will also be tension socially about the promotion of religion and its relation to freedom in this country and under our free speech rights.

Whatever the individual circumstances of each work environment, I would simply share four points to consider. First, after ordination, a man *is* a deacon, twenty-four hours a day, seven days a week. To hide his ordination sounds as strange as hiding his wedding ring in public. Second, because he is now clergy, that does not mean he is compelled to be overtly "religious" wherever he goes. One does not have to be continually inviting people to faith or worship or into personal prayer. As husbands, we are not always mentioning our wives or how we love them or testifying to how marriage should be everyone's state in life and so on. Third, as people at work begin to learn of the deacon's state in life, the virtue of prudence dictates how, when, and to what extent he will counsel people at work or pray with them or set up off-worksite appointments. The key is to live in the truth of being a deacon and then prayerfully discern how best one might meet the spiritual needs of this colleague at work in a way that undermines neither the purposes of work nor one's role at work. Fourth, commonly, spiritual needs arise at work, but explicit faith-driven attention to these needs is best addressed after work. If the needs are not complicated or substantive (for example, a colleague asks for a blessing or for a simple prayer in light of an upcoming health appointment), these may be dispatched within the worksite itself. If even these small movements of faith expression are frowned upon, however, then it is best to meet with the person immediately after work or at another convenient time. A deacon should be prepared for the Holy Spirit to draw people to him at work and should plan ahead to address these situations before they begin to happen.

Neighborhood Ministry

Another aspect of ordination that one should prepare for in formation is the new way neighbors might perceive his role in the neighborhood. This is especially true if the deacon lives in the vicinity of his parish assignment. One's presence in the neighborhood or apartment complex is now a new dimension of life for a deacon, as a public person. Parishioners on a Sunday morning see him assisting at the altar and proclaiming the Gospel and preaching on his assigned days. These people will recognize the deacon as he cuts the grass, shops in the grocery store, and watches his kids play basketball in the school gym. Meanwhile, he may know only a fraction of them.

It may become commonplace to have a dad slide down the bleachers in the school gym and ask for prayers or seek counsel about a family or work problem. Being ready to respond to these persons' vulnerability is part of the gift of generosity that a man should pray for as he lies upon the floor in the cathedral on ordination day. It is also true that, many times, the deacon's wife will be an envoy, operating between a person having a conversation with her in the grocery store and this same person's appearance before her husband in that grocery store's beer aisle seeking a prayer or blessing. Such availability to persons seeking Christ or relief from common burdens through shared prayer marks a man as a deacon. Acting out of such generous availability is why a man is "wounded" or "opened" at his ordination to receive Christ's own servant virtues.

That these virtues are Christ's indicates how close a deacon must remain to Christ in contemplative prayer to forestall any resentment toward people presenting their needs at inopportune times. The deacon also must stay close to Christ, calling upon grace to stymie the temptation to retreat, in nostalgia, to a life of anonymity. On our own, we "can do nothing" (Jn 15:5). Receiving the grace of Christ's own dedication to host the spiritual and corporal needs of others is a deacon's regular petitionary prayer. Also, recommitting oneself to a life of relational prayer is the only way a deacon can remain faithful to ministry from ordination to grave. Without this explicit communion with Christ in relational prayer, telling Christ all one's thoughts, feelings, and desires, it is not unusual to find oneself tempted to resent "needy" people. By neglecting prayer, a deacon can rouse anew a previous selfishness or escapism that he once thought had passed from his character. After ordination, a man still must be vigilant, protecting his prayerful communion with God, which enables him to give himself to those who cannot return in kind.

Although ministry in one's neighborhood can become a burden, there is the surprising joy one experiences in being able to preach Christ to those who live so close to home. This surprising joy becomes the content of one's evening prayer and examination of consciousness each night. In treasuring this aspect of ministry, one grows in gratitude for being called to such a vocation. It is gratitude that is at the heart of worship and is the accelerant to deepening our desire to pray. To be known locally as the man who prays, the man with whom one can pray, is truly an honor not to be taken for granted.

Daily Worship at the Parish

Attending daily worship is a great aid for a deacon and his wife to resist the temptation to "move back" and inhabit the land of popular American culture. We do not want merely to visit the land of the Eucharist; we want to dwell there. Daily worship is ordered according to our family and work duties. Nevertheless, it is equally vital to discern whether some sacrifices can be made so that daily worship can be accomplished. Christ wants to unleash this desire in us, and He will fulfill it as well.

As noted earlier, all deacons should place themselves in the presence of the Eucharist, either assisting at Mass or spending time in adoration, at least once a day. Will his family or work commitments allow this? It is a good question to ponder as one enters formation or even applies for acceptance into a formation program. If the man cannot assist at daily Mass regularly, will he seek out Eucharistic adoration? Within adoration, one could easily accomplish the duties of praying the Liturgy of the Hours and spending time in *lectio divina* as well. This question of worship is so vital that one should make it a common conversation with one's spiritual director. Obviously, if both spouses can enter a deeper Eucharistic life together, all the better for building a life of common love between each other and God. Such Eucharistic devotion can become a new facet of married love and faith.

Beyond Eucharistic devotion, can a deacon and his wife daily enter together into either morning or evening prayer, or both? This can be accomplished before the Blessed Sacrament at the parish church or in the living room while the children are calm or after they are asleep. The reality of a couple's prayer life during and after formation should be a regular topic of conversation so that their prayer life can be rightfully adjusted through the many seasons of family life.

The Role of Spiritual Direction in a Deacon's Prayer and Marriage

I have mentioned spiritual direction several times in this book, so I will close this chapter with a few comments on its necessity, meaning, and spiritual power.

Spiritual direction is a conversation one enters with a person who has been committed to his or her own personal prayer life, has theological education, and has completed a program of training explicitly to minister as a spiritual director. Further, such a director should hold orthodoxy as his or her standard of thinking. No deacon or his wife should be in direction with a person who dissents from the settled doctrine of the Catholic Church or is a person of partisan prejudice. One's director should be Catholic, orthodox, and possessing a mind formed by the Liturgy and the *Catechism*, not a political or philosophical ideology.

When beginning direction, a man in formation and his spouse should seek a director who sees direction itself as an experience of prayer. The role of the director is to create an environment wherein one can better listen to God within one's heart and mind. The director establishes himself or herself as one who carries a simple question: "What has the Most Holy Trinity been doing in your prayer lately?" As the deacon and his wife begin to share this activity of God in their lives with the director, they realize that direction allows them to recall (or better, experience afresh) how God has been loving them. The prerequisite for any fruitful spiritual-direction session is noticing one's own affective movements (e.g., I feel alone, loved, peaceful, etc.) and how one has related these to God in prayer. The director assists in discerning what movements, ideas, inspirations, or desires may be from God, which ones are simply our own, or even which ones contain interference from Satan. It is spiritual direction that invites us to mature in noticing our own interiority, that is becoming receptive to God loving us. Internalizing this love we live in communion with God, thinking and deciding out of this communion as well. As people of faith, we do not want to think, choose, feel, or desire in isolation from God. Remaining in communion with God, who is love and truth, is the way of holiness and sanity.

Prayer is God reaching us with His love. As Benedict XVI noted, "Prayer is pure receptivity."* God's perennial stance toward us is self-giving love. What makes prayer a chore at times is that we can "harden" ourselves against His outpouring of love. To pass through periods of such hardening is to know what it means to need a savior. This hardening devolves into all sorts of self-imposed sufferings, which may layer our days in darkness instead of light, creativity, and joy. Spiritual directors notice such

* Homily of His Holiness Benedict XVI at Randwick Racecourse, Sydney, Australia (July 20, 2008), Vatican.va.

stances within us and suggest ways to return to light. They do this primarily through one difficult suggestion: "I would invite you to remain with Jesus, to remain available to Him, and to be open to His initiatives of love." This is a difficult invitation because our default position as humans is to hide from God (Gn 3:10) and to choose instead our "own place" (Acts 1:25), eschewing the communion the Trinity offers us.

To make direction fruitful, we are invited to share all of what is happening in our hearts during the session itself. It is perfectly fine to stop the conversation and for both director and directee to enter into silence. It is vital for the directee to enter into this silence, listening for God's movement within. What we are listening for is the truth that needs to be said or explored. The director is inviting us to explore all interior content in our heart with God; *we never go into the heart alone*. Noticing what is happening in our heart *with God* ensures that our prayer and conversation with our director is lodged in reality. Only that which exists in reality can be related to God because reality is where He dwells.

It may take some time to come to prefer light, reality, and God to hiding, self, and immediate gratification. Directors are patient with our conversions; we need to be patient with ourselves as we take one step forward with each session. During our sessions, we especially want to explore any areas of difficulty or any graces we are receiving in faith, hope, and love. We want to discuss whether our prayer has become routine, heavy, or "false," or whether our mood toward people in our lives has shifted from something hospitable to something resentful or judgmental. We want to come to recognize any tendencies toward emotional isolation (e.g., "I am alone in my prayer; no one is listening" or "I am alone in my life "or "No one cares"). To push against any isolation or desolation in prayer is primary to spiritual growth, and directors want to hear about these situations when they occur.

It can be fruitful to take notes about our prayer times and

bring these to direction. Our memories are not that strong, and the graces God shares are multiple. His graces are subtle, and our memories are weak. This dynamic between the subtlety of grace and our weak memories can be seen in our own marriages. One spouse may claim in an argument to have "never" received love from the other. In fact, the "offending" spouse then might recount numerous incidents of very concrete expressions of love. The offended one has "forgotten" those expressions, or emotion has clouded the memory of them. Either way, false barriers are set up that threaten communion because our memories are weak. This can happen in our prayer as well. "Where are You, God? Why don't You love me?" But, in fact, He is close; and if we were to record His movements, we would know that His consolation is liberally given, though subtle, quiet, deep, and sustained. Keeping a prayer journal can aid our memory to retain a history of being loved. It is not necessary to record our prayer times, but it is certainly valid for those who know they will want to recall all that God is doing in their lives.

Since God is the God of our whole lives, it is legitimate to raise issues from our marriage that touch upon our prayer life or our vocation to become a deacon (or be married to one). The director is not a marriage counselor, so one ought to keep one's discussion about marriage within the purview of prayer or vocational discernment to the clerical life.

Having a spiritual director is a real blessing during formation for the diaconate. Most dioceses assign a director to a new candidate, but one should never be shy about reporting to the formation team if the assigned director is not assisting in the deepening of one's prayer life. This quality of assisting a candidate in deepening his prayer life is the *only one* that matters in the relationship with a spiritual director.

CHAPTER 4

Welcoming Holy Orders into the Family

Welcoming holy orders into a sacramental marriage is not the usual trajectory of most Catholic marriages. The norm is to welcome children, not another vocational sacrament, into the spousal communion. But in this unusual circumstance, another sacrament for the husband, holy orders, is welcomed into the family as a further way of being a communion of love and life — that is, marriage. Fatherhood and motherhood are the crown of spousal love. In the birth of children, the gift of husband given to wife and wife to husband is revealed. Beyond the gift of life that is children, a marriage also communicates spiritual, emotional, and intellectual life between the spouses. Here, the spouses receive "life" from one another as they present themselves to each other as gift. Their human dignity is secured, and their personalities affectively thrive in light of being beheld, chosen, and received in love by another.

Within this life-giving exchange of communication, commitment, and sexuality comes the gift of children. From the love of two strangers who have become friends and then spouses, helpmates to God, comes the enfleshed fruit of their love. From love comes more love and life, along with the challenge and blessing of being hospitable to all this love and life. Marriage and parenting can be an overwhelming flood of life, but it is also an opportunity to rectify the Fall of humankind, in a manner of speaking. In marriage, the ease humans know with self-involvement is countered by the beautiful suffering that is self-donative love toward spouse and offspring. Making room for the "other" (one's spouse and one's children) is truly a remedy for self-centered living, an occasion for drawing us more deeply into our identity as being made in the image and likeness of God. God is the very opposite of self-involvement. Spousal love and parenting stretch persons beyond what is preferable and self-satisfying and open them to a life of sustained regard for others. Such giving is recognized as one's highest dignity but also one's most difficult commitment.

And within this mystery of attraction and regard for others comes another call to a couple. This time, the couple is bidden to host within their spousal commitment a concrete ministerial aspect of the mystery of Christ, an aspect that marks a man for public witness and liturgical proclamation. It also defines his wife as one who consents to such a mission within her marriage and family.

What Does It Mean to Welcome the Diaconate into Spousal Love and Parenting?

To welcome Holy Orders into a marriage means that Christ's own ministry becomes internalized within the husband. It means that a husband's sharing in Christ's own diaconate is now a permanent reality within the marriage and family. Further, it means that such a husband, by the very definition of his "sharing in" Christ's own envoy-servant mission, reaches a new level of fidelity as a husband. Yes, welcoming the diaconate into a marriage must mean that the husband becomes a better husband — not first a better public figure or a more active ecclesiastical presence, but, first and foremost, he becomes a better image of Christ loving His Bride, the Church. For the deacon, the closest member of that Church is his own wife. The diaconate only threatens the communion of spouses if the husband or the communion itself were already dysfunctional. Only an unconverted or spiritually and emotionally immature man would see the diaconate as an altar upon which he sacrifices his marriage.

To have a deacon who is married ministering within the confines of a parish is first and foremost a gift to all the marriages in that parish. This gift is to be found in the couple's witness to the absolute necessity of integrating Eucharistic worship with sacramental marriage. Even if the deacon and his wife never exercise a concrete ministry to married or engaged couples, their presence is a witness to grace. If they do assist in strengthening or forming couples for marriage, all the better for the goals a pastor wishes to accomplish. The pastor has interests in assisting the deacon to integrate the envoy-servant mission of Christ in his own body in a way that secures fidelity to both wife and ministry. The theologically and spiritually mature pastor knows that the deacon is not "his" to summon as a convenience to lighten his own ministerial load. When the bishop sends a deacon to the pastor, it is an occasion for pastor and deacon and wife to sit down and communicate limits, hopes, dreams, and desires. This communication envisions how the deacon can help further the Gospel within the parish, all the while deepening his own bond with his wife and children. Only in the kind of relationship with a pastor that welcomes such communication should a wife entrust her husband and family to clerical ministry. And the bishop should entrust a married deacon only to a parish overseen by a pastor who wishes to base his relationship with the deacon upon this kind of open and emotionally mature virtue of communication.

Making Room for Mystery

When I use the word *mystery*, I am trying to indicate that the marriage is about to receive something that one is taken up into but that can never be fully understood. The mystery of Christ's love for His Bride, the Church, integrating with Christ's own ministry of envoy-service, can be lived but not fully grasped in its depth or substance. This makes sense because such mysteries are about and from God. Still, we live within sacraments, and over the course of our lives, we become more vulnerable to their meaning. Sacraments are the true content of our lives. To live in a sacrament (*mysterion*, from the Greek) is to be ushered safely into heaven when this life has ended. To live a life wherein the mystery of marriage is now enlarged to welcome the servant mysteries of Christ in the so configured body of the husband is to enter a deeper participation in all the previously received sacraments. More is added, nothing subtracted. The sacramental life is one hidden with Christ. It is a life so vulnerable to the dynamism of the Spirit that, over the years, one becomes another Christ (see Rom 8:29). As Catholics reach spiritual maturity, they reflect their union with Christ in thought, word, and action. We are, in a real way, mistaken for Christ. We call this holiness, sanctity, and a few of these other Christs who are known to be worthy of veneration even become canonized saints. Each sacrament received allows some aspect of the mystery of Christ's own life to inhabit us, and where we place no obstacle (sin) to this indwelling, he readily forms us into his "likeness" (Gn 1:26).

For a woman to welcome the diaconate into her marriage is to have her own life energized with wonder. "What more of Your life will You involve me in, Christ?" In our lives, we live moments of death and resurrection and service. With each opportunity to die to self or serve or come to new life through healing or choices to love and forgive, we aggregate to ourselves these aspects of Christ. To be the wife of a deacon is to be a woman who is free in her own identity as spouse and mother and more. The Church does not ask the wife to be a co-minister with her husband or to take on leadership roles in the parish. These or other ecclesial roles are not connected to being married to a deacon. These roles, if appropriated, flow from the woman's own baptism, natural gifts, and interests.

Minimally, the Church asks a wife only to give consent to having her husband become a deacon. What does this *consent* mean? To give consent is to *feel together* the reality that one's spouse has been chosen by Christ to host His envoy-servant mystery in his body. The wife and husband are expected to be of one mind on this integration of vocations. How should this consent be lived out in the marriage? First, I would say that such consent invites a true communication in discerning how the diaconate will be welcomed within the spousal communion.

Parameters should be agreed upon in service of integrating both the communion of spouses and the demands of prayer and ministry that are the diaconate. We are tempted to take the "easy" way and give ascendency to either the commitment of marriage or the duties of the diaconate. But this will not honor both vocations. Elevating one over the other only lays open the possibility that one commitment may be neglected. Integration is the key to this new life, not ascendency or balance. In balancing something, we try to make things equal in time, duties, and commitments. A marriage hosting the diaconate is not about balance but about a continual communication between spouses in service of making the marriage and diaconate a *whole*. This new life is not lived faithfully by carving it into parts but by imagining it lived as a whole, imagining the life lived together anew. The marriage is not the enemy of the diaconate, and the diaconate does not threaten spousal communion. Both are simply the new way we live as one, as a couple. Of course, one or the other could become a threat to this complementarity, but that is usually due to some human weakness or unhealed wounds that preexisted the entry of the diaconate into the marriage. When insecurity or lack of communication or family-of-origin wounds are not attended to within the marriage, then, yes, the diaconate can appear as a threat.

This is why it is so crucial to accept into formation only men who exist in a strong and emotionally healthy marriage. We cannot integrate the diaconate into a faulty marital system. Is the couple working together? Are they in a network of communication that is so open that each one knows the other, his or her needs, strengths, fears, virtues, and so on? Or is the marital system not connecting? Do the spouses exist in the same location but without their communion thriving? Have they failed to internalize one another through conversation that bears fruit as intimacy?

Consent, then, is a larger issue than simply asking a wife to "add one more thing" to the calendar. It is her praying about and imagining her current communion with her spouse. Is it secure enough to become the foundation for an entirely new way of life? Cautious discernment is a must, and a wife should withhold her consent if she knows that the diaconate is the next "achievement" on her husband's list. Such a list is kept because the husband is still reckoning his identity as flowing from his accomplishments. Instead, sound Catholic doctrine teaches that one's identity is bestowed in communion with wife and God. No wife should send her husband on the mission of diaconal witness if she knows he still possesses an identity built upon résumé padding. Only a marriage that stands upon the strength of *a communion of distinct persons who have become a whole* can develop into a new whole by hosting the diaconate. Without such strength, the marriage will be measured in parts, birthing rivalries and leading to threats. The diaconate and marriage will become competitors over time and space.

Making Room for Children's Formation

Sometimes after ordination to the diaconate, a man's children — those in college or who have moved out of the house — choose not to worship anymore, drifting from the spiritual traditions that a deacon and his wife have faithfully passed on. There is no guarantee that ordination will bring religious unity within a family. This disunity is a source of great sadness to the deacon and his wife. Trying to pass on the faith to children is one of the great duties of discipleship in a Catholic marriage; but, of course, each child receives the evangelizing parent in a unique way, influenced by personality, cultural and educational environments, psychological wounds, peer influence, and the moral and personality weaknesses of the parents themselves. Becoming a believer is the mystery of freedom meeting invitation. Sometimes the invitation is rejected.

Each Catholic couple, however, welcomes a new baby and is eager to have that child baptized into the mystery of Christ's love. The couple strives to incorporate the child into whatever level of faith is present in them. Ironically, some very faithful couples find their children rejecting the Faith, and some more laissez-faire couples may witness their children becoming quite fervent in belief. One thing we have certainty of is that there is no one formula that guarantees the transmission of faith to the next generation. There are many theories and books promoting certain methods for evangelizing children within the home, but none of these is foolproof. They carry good advice: Teach your children to pray; pray with them; teach them the Rosary; bring them to Eucharistic adoration; read and pray with Scripture in the home; attend Sunday Mass; practice the spiritual and corporal works of mercy;

invite priests and religious to your home for dinner; encourage your children to read age-appropriate books on the Faith or the saints; register your children for youth group or catechesis; look for opportunities to send your children to faith-based camps or on faith-based hiking trips; attend large youth rallies that expose your children to many thousands of young Catholics at once; sign up for youth retreats; volunteer at the parish; when college age arrives, encourage your children to live at the Catholic Newman Center or attend its activities; and so on.

Yes, the Faith may be passed on if such commitment is part of your family life, but if it is not passed on, only a small bit of soul-searching may be necessary. Do not get caught in a cycle of self-condemnation. This is especially wasteful and spiritually harmful when your own children do not know why they left the Church when questioned about it. At that point, the following advice is not piety clothed in despair but an act of tapping into true supernatural power: Pray and sacrifice for your children's return to the Church. This prayer and sacrifice may last many decades, but we stretch out to God in hope, knowing that He wants their return to worship even more than we do. Many testimonies reveal that children return to the Faith not on their parents' timetable but on God's. It may be after we have been long dead, but what we want most is for our children to return to the Faith before their own deaths. Such is the power of prayer.

For those parents who practice all or part of the good advice above and sense that the Faith seems to have been welcomed by their children, it is now time to invite them to welcome something else: Dad's diaconate. How should this be done? Inculcating hospitality toward the diaconate in a child's mind and heart is easier in younger children. Very young children who are already being taught to pray with Mom and Dad and attend church with them can more readily absorb the fact that "Daddy is going to be at the altar with Father someday too." This is more difficult to accept in many a self-conscious, insecure, and identity-seeking teenager. For younger children, Dad's diaconate will be organic. They have only known Dad to be a deacon; *Dad* and *deacon* are synonymous to them. It might be helpful to show the children photos of deacons, talk about how Daddy will now vest himself at Mass and that he will be at the altar and no longer sitting with the family. It may even be helpful to bring the children to church when it is empty and give them a tour of where Daddy will be sitting, where he will stand at the altar, where he will proclaim the Gospel from this "big book" while standing in the ambo. Also, Daddy must be welcoming to the people of the parish after Mass, greet them, and even pray with them before all the families go home. Opening this new routine for the children at Mass will concretize the change they and their friends will see each Sunday regarding Dad's new vocation. Slowly, Dad's other ministries can be introduced. Dad will not be home tonight; he is teaching Order of Christian Initiation of Adults (OCIA); or he is needed by a sick person; or a young couple is about to get married, and Dad is helping them understand their life together; and so forth.

Such new behaviors may cause some confusion on the part of the children, but their sacrifice must be noted, and consolation must be extended if Dad's absence causes some sadness. Obviously, making children sacrifice like this is why some counsel that no man with young children in the home should be ordained. If the diaconal ministry is proportioned, however, and the deacon receives his affirmation from contemplative prayer, his wife, and his children, then saying no to excessive ministerial commitments is easier. Emotional harm to the children of deacons is incurred when the deacon dad is miserly in communication with them or is emotionally immature. This immaturity, as mentioned earlier, is expressed by his identity being lodged in function, achievement, and busyness. Deacons, as envoy-servants configured to Christ, may be needed in many places, but each individual deacon is not.

Largely, raising small children in a diaconal family is like raising small children in any Catholic family. The young children simply grow up with Dad as a deacon. To them, Dad has always been a deacon. That is how his fatherhood is understood by them. In such a family, the Faith is passed on in the normal ways, as mentioned above. But for older children, having Dad become a deacon can be upsetting. If they are in middle school or high school, such a change in the family culture can be disturbing to their routine, expectations, and even self-understanding. Until now, they have known only private citizen Dad, Dad in the pew next to me, Dad in golf shirt and not Dad in vestments and at the altar and preaching publicly about Christ. This contrast of identities may be accepted slowly by teens. Their progressive acceptance is to be reverently respected by the parents, or the older children may resent the whole vocation of the deacon from the start. Heavy-handed promotion of the diaconate to older children who are shocked by its implications for family life will only sow the seeds of resentment.

It certainly is not the case that older children and teens get to sideline a man's call to holy orders, but their fears, surprise, and projected personal harm to their standing among peers must be attended to over time and intentionally. Now, of course, there are families in which the announcement of Dad's new vocation is received maturely and with great pride. The teen is on board from the beginning with the idea that Dad is entering holy orders. That kind of reaction is a blessing and not rare. But such a reaction is not universal.

How to Help Older Children Welcome the Diaconate into Their Family

Most teens are aware of their father's commitment to Catholicism well before he reveals to them that he wants to pursue formation in holy orders. Hopefully, this dad is a daily Mass attender, a leader in prayer in the home, and a volunteer at the parish in some organization or service activities. Perhaps his teens have found him praying with the Bible or reading spiritual books. So they should have a good idea that God is a major part of their father's life. Still, moving from a father who is committed to Christ as a layman to one wearing vestments and proclaiming the Gospel every Sunday is quite a disruption to the teenage mantra "above all, do not stand out as different." Certainly, approaching a teen with the news of Dad's interest in ordination should be an announcement carrying the seriousness it deserves. In other words, it should not be shared with the teen casually over the breakfast table, akin to someone sharing that he intends to join the Knights of Columbus. No, this announcement needs intentional space and time to be shared. The news needs to sink into the teen's mind and heart. This father, who went to work, cut the grass, watched football on television, and worshiped in church is now going to be a public figure around town. That could be a scary prospect for a teenager who once asked that she be dropped off at the movies a block away from the theater!

So Dad should call a family meeting and communicate as best he can several things: Why he wants to become a deacon; what this means for his presence around the house; how it will affect the activities of the children; what duties and responsibilities, if any, this will impose upon the children; what benefits he sees the diaconate bringing to family life; and how, in responding to this vocation, he foresees any development in his own character and behavior. It would be good at this point for the mother to share her experience of finding out about their dad's choice to pursue ordination. How did it affect her when she first found out? Why is she supporting this decision? What fears did she have at first that now appear to have been calmed over time? Were all her questions answered to her satisfaction, giving peace of heart? Give the teens permission to explore their feelings about this family event immediately within the family meeting, but also encourage them to bring their feelings and thoughts to an outside mentor they trust — a teacher, a counselor, a parish priest, or their favorite grandparent. To help them explain the new vocation to their peers, teens can simply relate that their father wants to be closer to God and this vocation will give him the opportunity to do so; or that he wants to deepen his service to the Church and this new vocation satisfies that desire. Simple answers will often be accepted by peers readily as they nod their heads and continue eating their lunch in the school cafeteria. Coming up with simple answers and seeing them received by peers helps one's daughter or son "get the news out" and then blend back into daily life.

As noted earlier, some teens have known teasing in response to their announcement that their dad will become a deacon. If not processed with the parents or other adults, such teasing can wound a teen and instill resentment toward the vocation. Inform the children that such teasing may be a possibility. Suggest that they tell those friends who are closest first and so experience their support and acceptance. The news of the vocation will spread, but by that time, the teen will have found the support needed to weather any snide comments from the peripheries ("Are you going to become a *priest* too, David?", etc.).

Reassure the teens that this family meeting is only the beginning of the conversation about the diaconate, and invite them to approach at any time with their questions, fears, and positive anticipations ("I think it will be cool to hear Dad preach on Sunday"). It would be good to end the meeting with family prayer as it is normally done in the home.

If, after much family conversation, consultation, and prayer, a teen still resists the idea that his or her father will become a deacon, one may slow the process of entering formation to see if any of the teen's concerns can be resolved. It may be that the dad goes forward into formation, inviting the teen to understand that his life choice does not *define the teen*. If the teen is concerned about peer rejection, it might be a good occasion to instruct the teen in fortitude, encourage him or her to develop a clear articulation of his or her own stance toward the dad's vocation and embrace the truth stated above: that a father's choice does not define or exhaust the meaning of a teen's life. This, of course, would be a very difficult family situation, but refusing to go ahead with formation after it has been discerned as a vocation would be to exchange a vocation for serving the fears of unhealed adolescent emotions.

Making Room for Spiritual Differences

In some families, it may be that not only the older children chafe against Dad's plan to seek ordination. Even though he received consent from his wife, she may wish to qualify her consent, considering her own way to God and her personal relationship with the Church. Ideally, a wife will receive the news of her husband's vocation with joy and even eager anticipation. She is proud of him for listening to God in this way. But some wives stress their independence from their husband's vocation. Such independence is not felt in any negative or resentful way but simply out of the clear awareness that this is "his" vocation; she already has one: wife, perhaps mother, often along with a profession. She is happy for her husband; she worships with him, supports, and listens to his discernment and formation experiences but does not find that his formation should also be hers. She has other founts of spiritual formation in service of her maturing conscience. Again, her independence is not a rejection of or rebellion against the diaconate. It is not a negative stance at all; it is simply her living her vocation. She may not be attracted to the way her husband prays or his public witness to the Church and doctrine. She may approach prayer through a different piety, or she may be more reticent to engage in public discourse about matters of faith. It may also be that she is more demonstrative than her husband regarding the Faith. So be it. Spouses are attracted to persons who are different from themselves, not those who are simply extensions of themselves.

Presuming the marriage is emotionally and morally sound, the husband already knows how to accommodate his wife's vision of integrating the diaconate into the marriage. I will share two simple observations. First, God approaches us as individuals. He reverences our freedom and our developmental progress in faith and spirituality. As spouses, we should do the same for one another. The union of the marriage is central, and our own spiritual approaches to prayer and devotional life serve to preserve both our communion with God and the marital union. These approaches may be unique to each spouse, but they ought not to be at odds with one another. In the end, a couple should be able to say, "In the ways we pray, together and alone, in the devotions we follow, together and alone, our union with one another and God is stronger." Is your union stronger? If it is, continue moving deeper into the spiritual lives that you are living, both as a couple and singularly. Do you sense any tension or threat or weakening of the union? If so, perhaps it is time to converse about what is being noticed. If necessary, seek advice from a pastoral leader or a spiritual director.

Even in reverencing a spouse's unique way to approach God, it can be fruitful to enter some prayer together. Of course, a wife may prefer Holy Hours while the husband prefers *lectio divina* or the Rosary or charismatic prayer or some other approach. As noted above, continue to enter these exercises as an individual. But can there be a common ground besides Sunday or daily Mass? Can compromise be reached to spend at least some moments together asking the Spirit to bless the marriage, the children, and the ministry? One agreed-upon spiritual practice might be to read Scripture together, either aloud or in silence, and then close with a brief intercessory prayer. Or the couple might agree to pray Night Prayer together from the Liturgy of the Hours. Exploring a common prayer explicitly brings you into the presence of God as a married couple, as the sacrament you are, a sign of Christ loving His Church. Strengthening knowledge of one's union with Christ through the union you have with one another in prayer furthers the intimacy of the marriage and deepens spousal love.

Another area in which a wife may wish to express her own way of living her faith is in her apostolic service. In some dioceses, it is traditional to refer to a married couple that has welcomed the diaconate into it as a "deacon couple." Again, in some dioceses, there is a public recognition upon ordination noting what "his" ministries and "her" ministries consist of, perhaps on the diocesan website or in the news or parish bulletins. Obviously, only the husband has become a deacon. There is no vocation called a "deacon couple." There is no expectation that the wife of a deacon must engage in any lay ministry, outside the norm of what baptism calls a layperson to do. Each wife should know that she is to engage in parish life as she wants to engage. Being a deacon's wife is not a ministry; it does not oblige any ministry, nor should there be any pressure upon the wife from her husband, her pastor, or wives of other deacons to think otherwise.

By grace, some women may sense a call from the Spirit to become more involved in diocesan or parish life, but this is simply a grace for *that* woman. It is a common witness that many wives have entered during diaconal formation and after the ordination of their husbands. It cannot, however, be universalized as a requirement of couples who welcome the diaconate into their marriage.

CHAPTER 5
The Real Presence

Since Catholic marriage images Christ loving His Church (Eph 5:25), the vocation must draw inspiration for behavior from the sacramental source of that reality. Couples are to examine their lives considering the example of Christ, who loved the Church and gave himself up for her. The reality of Christ's giving himself for His Bride is accessible each day in those areas of the world where Mass is celebrated regularly. Whether the couple participates in this "giving up" once a week or more often, they long for one effect in doing so: They want their spousal love to participate in Christ's own love of His Bride, and they want that participation to define their daily lives together. As Benedict XVI wrote, "Union with Christ is also union with all those to whom he gives himself. I cannot possess Christ just for myself; I can belong to him only in union with all those who have become, or who will become, his own."* And certainly, one's own Christian spouse is one of Christ's "own." When a man loves his wife, he is loving Christ. Marriage is a sacrament, and, hence, the

* *Deus Caritas Est* (December 25, 2005), Vatican.va, par. 14.

love between the spouses is simultaneously an encounter in love with Christ. It is He who has bound himself to the spouses — He who invites them to bind themselves to Him through sacramental marriage and the Eucharist.

The marriage bond is intrinsically linked to the Eucharist, as this bond represents Christ's own love of His Spouse until the end (see Jn 13:1). Conjugal love is a sacramental sign of Christ's love for His Church, a love culminating on the cross. The cross is the expression of His marriage to humanity, and at the same time, the origin and heart of the Eucharist.* God is seeking holy communion with us, and we are seeking the same with our spouses. Both marriage and the Eucharist are realities ordered toward communion through self-revelation and self-giving. Such vulnerability invites the response of the same. So, in marriage and in Mass, there is a reciprocity of love, an exchange of bodies as gift.

Spousal communication involves beholding ("I see you"), which leads to self-revelation, leading to encounter unto intimacy, leading to sustained communion, and finally, culminating in personal internalization on the part of the spouses. "I encounter you" becomes "I carry you within me." There is an inexorable movement in emotionally and spiritually healthy couples toward a union of persons that results in new life and mutual internalization of the beloved. Here, spousal love dimly mirrors what is being initiated at the Mass. God is seeking union with His Bride, taking her into himself for all eternity. Such a longing for union is prevented only by our free will to sin. Any such turning in on the self on the part of spouses also prevents union in a marriage. Conversion toward living in truth sets the foundation for both an ever-maturing marriage and an ever-maturing life of worship.

When spouses reveal the truth about themselves to each other, they begin and sustain a journey of life and live "more

* Benedict XVI, *The Eucharist*, 50–51.

abundantly" (Jn 10:10). One reveals and one responds in thanksgiving. Both marriage and the Eucharist involve the life-sharing communion of persons unto gratitude.

To be vulnerable to the presence of one's spouse, a presence made more real by communication, is to welcome the change this same presence brings to one's life. It is a change of heart that leads one to make the welfare of another one's priority. This presence draws out of the spouse a conversion from self-involvement to self-gift. Cultivating a consciousness of our spouse's presence guards us from taking her or him for granted. Such awareness assists the marriage to deepen and endure. To develop this grateful consciousness toward our spouse is analogous to our surrendering to and acknowledging that Christ is truly present to us at Mass. To lose consciousness of both our spouse and Christ the Savior, our vocation and duty to worship, would be to lose one's grasp on reality.

To live in the presence of the spouse does not mean that one lives in perpetual subjective satisfaction; suffering, boredom, nonchalance (lack of interest) will be known. Acknowledging this being in the presence of God and spouse as gift enables us to be vulnerable to them, to host a presence, to be affected by or be penetrated by this presence down to the source of our thoughts and emotions. This is what it means to be a spouse: I no longer think like a bachelor; I think like one who is *in communion*. This is true also of the Catholic at Mass. I no longer think like a citizen of the popular and political Western culture; I think like a native of the Liturgy.

Choosing to live in the presence of God and spouse carries one consistent, annoying temptation: We tend to want to reduce these presences to be servants of our self-interest. To look on marriage as a succession of self-satisfying events and Mass as entertainment is a regular temptation. To critique these sacramental presences according to such a standard is to stay entrapped in suffocating emotional and moral isolation. The point of noticing the real presence of God or one's spouse is to be beguiled by the other's beauty; it is to forget the self. In other words, slowly, developmentally, one enters communion with another and leaves self-involvement behind. Such attention to the other becomes communion, and as communion is achieved, one is gifted with interior peace. Egocentric agitation becomes muted.

Instead of such agitation, I come to realize that being with the other, God and spouse, is my form of being with myself.* Communion does not threaten the self; it confirms it, enlivens it, and preserves it. "Yet I live, no longer I, but Christ lives in me" (Gal 2:20).

Both worship and marriage invite us to *die to self*, not keeping the self sustained by the life support of egocentricity. Forgetting the self and hosting the other is how the self remains alive. It dies when it fears it must keep itself alive through self-centeredness.

So the Mass and marriage establish us in communion of presences, and through that, both the self and the other reach an existence of peace. Since we are still in a fallen world and sin is active as the enemy of such communion, we are also bidden to sacrifice to sustain that communion. We must fight to retain communion. We fight not with our puny wills, however, but in coordination with the supernatural power of Christ found in the paschal mystery. Our faith in the sacramental life is a call to become assimilated into Christ's own act of self-donation upon the Cross. This assimilation is possible as we worship at Mass. In such worship, surrender, and gratitude, we are enabled by grace to serve the needs of our spouse, as Christ did for His.

Over the years of receiving Christ in the Eucharist, listening to Him in the proclaimed Gospel, and surrendering our lives to Him at the Offertory and the Consecration, we become assimilated to Him; that is, we lose ourselves in the action of Christ

* Joseph Ratzinger, "Concerning the Notion of Person in Theology," *Communio* 17 (Fall 1990): 451.

upon the cross. "I surrender to You, Christ. Take me up *into that kind of love, the kind that only You can attain.*" Over the decades of worship, we have only one goal: "He must increase; I must decrease" (Jn 3:30). Couples that inhabit the Liturgy become men and women who live and choose and think and feel out of the power of regularly receiving Christ's own life and love into their bodies and souls. They want to love out of the love of Christ that now defines their interior lives. They no longer believe their own will is strong enough to love in the way they are called to by the sacramental life. They must continue to diminish their own agendas and let the life of Christ and their communion with Him be the norm for how they orient their lives. The Eucharist is alive, not inert; and it must become alive in the marriages of deacons and their wives. At Mass, we receive the love that is His, thus becoming able to sacrifice the life that is ours for the welfare of our spouses.

We need to share in Christ's life to love our spouses faithfully because "in the beginning" (Gn 1:1), instead of marrying God, we espoused ourselves to sin. Sin is the opposite of the sacrifice of the Mass and of marriage: It is the refusal of self-gift. Sin uses reality to serve the immediate needs of one's selfish self. Sin is the opposite of the generosity of the cross, and so, to subvert sin, the God-Man, Jesus, makes himself a gift.[†]

Spouses' making themselves gifts to one another is the truth of what marriage in Christ means. Together, in marriage, the couple chooses to reciprocate love, anticipate needs, and mutually sacrifice self-involvement in service to their union of persons. The couple forms a dynamic, reciprocal whole; their communion is really a way of being a gift to one another. They are one in their mutual self-giving. Such giving *is* their unity. They also complement one another in their differences.

† For more on Christ's making himself a gift, see the essay by Michael Heintz, "An Encounter with the Word Made Flesh: Louis Bouyer on Eucharistic Communion," *Gregorianum* 95, no. 4 (2014): 677–98.

The woman is the helpmate in the things of God (Gn 2:18). Primarily, she reorients the man toward communion if his natural desire to look outward and solve problems makes him veer off course relationally with God and others. Alternately, the man invites the woman to expand her vision when her world is conflated into relations, when she is absorbed by relations and loses her own identity.

Spouses are the keepers of desires, their own and, when growing faint, their spouses'. Our desires need to be great because God revealed that we were created for greatness: sharing in His own love for all eternity. Nothing great ever comes about without great desire. Our greatest desire, then, is holy communion ("God alone satisfies" [CCC 1718]). It fulfills our need, our nature. We are relational beings. But our spouses cannot be the end of our desire for communion, even though such communion is very good. We are ordered toward *more* than our spouse: We are ordered toward eternal rest in communion with God.

Our lives are a pilgrimage of purification. We move from desiring what gives us pleasure to desiring the source of that pleasure and goodness, the very person. We move from choosing what is simply in our immediate self-interest to choosing what is good. Such is the journey of Christian maturity. So much of life is repenting for choosing to please the self rather than securing the communion we are offered with a *person*. In the end, as in Christ's own life, our purified desires are meant to order us toward *giving* the *self*, not taking in service of self-interest.

Such emphasis upon self-giving can raise fears in us. We become tempted to return to self-reliance in service of self-centeredness as we wonder, "If I give myself away to God or spouse, who will think of me? What about my needs?" The mystery revealed by Divine Love refutes this fear. By this revelation, we learn that the closer we come to God, the more *we give ourselves*, the more, in fact, *we become ourselves*. We do not lose the self by giving it away; we gain it. We receive our identity. We enter a mutual reciprocity of self-donation with our spouses, a mutual giving, flowing from the source of such giving itself, the Holy Trinity. We access this source in the Mass, and it flows through us if we keep inviting it to do so.

At worship, we come to know both a deepened gratitude for our spouses and the knowledge that we are to hold their presence lightly (not absolutely), as death will usher us into the *Source* of our spouses' life and beauty. God is this Source of life and love; our spouses are not. Our spouses simply reflect the Source's desire for us, God's own desire to marry humanity. Both wife and husband experience a glimpse into this tension — into the spouse's being the *reflection* of God and not God — when, as deacon, the husband leaves the side of his wife (relative good, reflection) to enter the sanctuary (heaven, source of love and life). And yet, ultimately, the husband and wife will be reunited in their mutual communion with God, not as spouses, but as members of the Body of Christ. Even at the Mass, this ultimate unity in Christ is glimpsed when the deacon husband comes from the sanctuary to give his wife holy Communion. What unites them now, union with the mysteries of Christ, will be what unites them eternally.

Catholic marriage is a journey of purification, gratitude, conversion, and worship. The spouses prepare one another to allow God to be all in all, to penetrate to the heart, and thus, to have that heart survive death and live on in the very source of that married love. This mystery is encountered and secured in the Mass, in which each spouse is taken up into the very spousal self-giving of the Bridegroom toward the Bride. We are called to behold both the Person of God and our spouses in love and gratitude. In worship of God, we are called to contemplate Him (in the actions and person of Christ) and empty ourselves of idols.

In the "worship" of our spouses, we are called to behold them and empty ourselves of those selfish distractions that keep us from remaining in our spouses' real presence. The word *worship* can be applied to the reverence given to a wife because her beauty and presence elicit in the man an acknowledgment of her "worth," and the same can be said of the reverence a wife gives her husband. To remain in the presence of one's spouse is both to recognize the spouse as a gift and to act toward him or her by offering one's presence in return.

As spouses and Christians, deacons are called to lives of bodily self-surrender in response to the bodily self-surrender to them of both spouse and God. As God and man were one in Christ's body, we, as humans, now have a hope to live a similar life, one infused with the divine life. Christ wants to give us this. We need to give ourselves to Christ through our gift of self to our spouse (sacrament), the poor (mission), and God himself upon the altar (worship). In turn, God will continue to give us all we have ever desired but that has taken a life's journey to believe: All I have ever wanted was *You.*

In the Eucharist, our deepest desire to be perfectly loved by God receives a promise from God that such love to rest in will be given. In the Eucharist, we receive a second sign that the hope for perfect love as a spouse will not go unsatisfied either. In Christ, the presence of our spouses to us will go on as well. Because of the life, death, and resurrection of Christ, there is a reasonable belief that such a love as I have for my spouse, such a force of life and communion, will not be extinguished by death. Life and love go on.

Conclusion

A married deacon, with his wife and family, gives witness to the sanctity of marriage. The more the deacon and his spouse grow in mutual love, conforming their lives to the Church's teaching on marriage and sexuality, the more they give to the Christian community a model of Christlike love, compassion, and self-sacrifice. The married deacon must always remember that through his sacramental participation in both vocational sacraments, first in matrimony and again in holy orders, he is challenged to be faithful to both. With integrity, he must live out both sacraments in harmony and balance.*

To enter holy orders after one has already pledged a lifetime of love to one woman is a surprise of the first order! Most men cannot see that such a vocation will be offered to them by Christ and His Church in the early years of being sacramentally married. But as the couple's married love, faith, and service mature, the man notices that, within all those venues of self-giving, an-

* *National Directory for the Formation, Ministry, and Life of Permanent Deacons in the United States*, 2nd ed., par. 74.

other form of giving, imbued with Christ's spirit of service, is being invited. Accepting the invitation to enter holy orders in cooperation with the vital and generous consent of one's spouse is truly a blessing and a challenge for spousal union. To live this integrated vocation with joy and fidelity is a true service to the Church and a witness to any children born of this love that Christ is, indeed, faithful, and following Him is a spiritual and moral adventure. "I came so that they might have life and have it more abundantly" (Jn 10:10). Such words are particularly apt for that couple who consents to host within their love for one another the envoy-servant mysteries of Christ.

About the Author

Deacon James Keating, Ph.D., is professor of spiritual theology at Kenrick-Glennon Seminary in Saint Louis, Missouri. He was formerly director of deacon formation for the Archdiocese of Omaha. He is married to Marianne, and they have four children and five grandchildren.

OSV

OSV